SOCIETY FOR NEW TESTAMENT STUDIES
MONOGRAPH SERIES

GENERAL EDITOR
MATTHEW BLACK, D.D., F.B.A.

19

THE PASSION NARRATIVE OF ST LUKE

THE PASSION NARRATIVE
OF ST LUKE

A CRITICAL AND HISTORICAL
INVESTIGATION

BY

VINCENT TAYLOR

EDITED BY

OWEN E. EVANS

Lecturer in Biblical Studies
University College of North Wales, Bangor

CAMBRIDGE
AT THE UNIVERSITY PRESS
1972

Published by the Syndics of the Cambridge University Press
Bentley House, 200 Euston Road, London NW1 2DB
American Branch: 32 East 57th Street, New York, N.Y.10022

© Cambridge University Press 1972

Library of Congress Catalogue Card Number: 79-163057

ISBN: 0 521 08295 1

Printed in Great Britain
at the University Printing House, Cambridge
(Brooke Crutchley, University Printer)

CONTENTS

PREFACE

In 1926, stimulated by B. H. Streeter's article in the *Hibbert Journal* for October 1921 on the Proto-Luke hypothesis and later by his classic work, *The Four Gospels*, published in 1924, I wrote *Behind the Third Gospel*, which was published as a thesis by the Clarendon Press of Oxford. When first announced, this hypothesis was received with very considerable favour, but later, largely in consequence of the searching criticisms of J. M. Creed in his *Commentary on Luke* (1930) and those of J. W. Hunkin in an article in the *Journal of Theological Studies* (April 1927, pp. 250–62), it lost ground in critical opinion. Owing to competing interests in form criticism and in biblical theology and to the decline of interest in literary criticism it continued to lose favour. It reached the nadir of its fortunes in A. R. C. Leaney's *Commentary on Luke* (1958), where it is dismissed in six lines as unsound with no argument except the unsupported claim that Proto-Luke's 'lack of either an Apocalypse or a Passion Narrative would deprive it of all claim to be called a gospel'.

The situation as it existed in 1951 was well described by A. M. Hunter in his book, *Interpreting the New Testament*. 'The hypothesis', he wrote, 'remains hypothetical.' It had not been disproved, but certain pillars on which it rested had weakened under criticism, and few scholars were prepared in constructive work to commit themselves to its truth. The hypothesis, he said, was not only interesting, but important, since, if established, we should have in Proto-Luke an authority for the life of Jesus as old as Mark, independent of it, and of comparable value; and he expressed the hope that in the next decade or two we might have a decision one way or the other from scholars 'ready to undertake the linguistic spade-work which such a decision will involve'. It is interesting to observe that at the very time Professor Hunter was writing, spades – one might say excavators – were already busy in Germany, at Göttingen and Münster, in the hands of J. Jeremias, H. Schürmann, and F. Rehkopf.

vii

In *The Eucharistic Words of Jesus* (which first appeared in English in 1955) and in an important article in *New Testament Studies* entitled 'Perikopen-Umstellungen bei Lukas' ('Luke's Alterations of the Position of Narratives') (IV (Jan. 1958), 115–19), Jeremias affirmed that, except in Lk. vi. 17–19 and viii. 19–21, Luke retains Mark's arrangement of the material most faithfully until we come to the Passion narrative, and that therefore, in contrast with Matthew, Luke is 'an enemy of rearrangement'. He lists six changes of order in Lk. xxii, and says that if Luke followed Mark in the crucifixion story, the material has been completely 'mixed up' (*durcheinandergewirbelt*). Schürmann's monumental work, *Quellenkritische Untersuchung des lukanischen Abendmahlsberichtes Lk. xxii. 7–38*, followed in 1953–7; in it he examined in the greatest detail the linguistic characteristics of this part of the Passion narrative, and Rehkopf did the same as regards Lk. xxii. 21–3 and 47–53 in *Die lukanische Sonderquelle, Ihr Umfang und Sprachgebrauch* in 1959. Some account of these works will be given later. Meantime it may be said that each of these scholars has accepted in substance the truth of the Proto-Luke hypothesis. It seems timely therefore to ask that British scholars should re-examine this hypothesis. I intend in what follows to attempt to do this with special attention to the Lukan Passion narrative. I do not propose to examine the whole of the Proto-Luke hypothesis, for its opponents, especially J. M. Creed and J. W. Hunkin, the most important, long ago admitted that Luke had already combined Q and L, that is, the sayings-document and the special Lukan tradition, before he wrote his Gospel, while maintaining that the Passion narrative in Luke is an edited version of Mark's account and that Mark supplies the framework of the Third Gospel. It is, moreover, to the Passion narrative that the three German scholars mentioned above have directed their attention. If they are right, the Proto-Luke hypothesis is established, although reconsideration must be given to the question of the influence of Mark on Luke. Such questions as the Markan or non-Markan character of Lk. vi. 17–19 remain for study, and it is possible that upon these issues critical opinion will continue to be divided. The nature, however, of Lk. vi. 17–19 is not a decisive issue, since no matter whether Luke drew this narrative from his special source or whether he transposed Mk. iii. 7–12 (= Lk. vi. 17–19) and Mk. iii. 13–19 (the appointment of the Twelve), in order to introduce the Sermon, does not seriously affect the hypothesis.

Later I shall discuss the methods by which the Passion narrative must be examined, the chief difference in my approach being a greater use of linguistic arguments than was made in *Behind the Third Gospel*. In this endeavour I am strongly indebted to the labours of Schürmann and Rehkopf, an account of whose work I have supplied in two articles in the *Expository Times* (LXXIV, 77–81 and 262–6) and an article on Rehkopf's list of words and phrases illustrative of pre-Lukan speech-usage in the *Journal of Theological Studies* (New Series XV, 59–62). To the Editors of these learned journals I am indebted for permission to draw upon these articles. I feel this investigation to be necessary on my part since *Behind the Third Gospel* has been out of print for some time, and especially because I have read and weighed all the criticisms and objections against the Proto-Luke hypothesis which have come to my notice since 1926, and to which in some cases I have replied in various articles. In the main I have felt an increased confidence in the early existence of the Lukan Passion narrative, but in deference to the opinions of other writers I have modified my earlier views in some respects. These changes concern (1) the manner and extent to which Luke was influenced by the Markan Passion narrative, and (2) the signs of still earlier stages in Luke's account of the Passion and resurrection. I have noted especially C. H. Dodd's observation, coupled with his acceptance of Streeter's hypothesis, that 'we do not know what amount of revision "proto-Luke" underwent in being incorporated in the Third Gospel' (see below, p. 9). In substance I have re-affirmed, and still further supported, the views expressed in *Behind the Third Gospel*. I believe the early existence of a pre-Lukan Passion source to be a matter of first importance since it enables us to reach back almost a generation to the accounts which the first Christians preserved of the death and resurrection of Jesus.

VINCENT TAYLOR

EDITORIAL NOTE

The present work contains the late Dr Vincent Taylor's last contribution to New Testament scholarship. He worked on it over a period of almost four years, from early 1962 to late 1965. Failing health, however, prevented him from finally revising the manuscript in preparation for publication, with the result that it lay untouched until after Dr Taylor's death in November 1968. Encouraged by several New Testament scholars who had long felt the need for a revised edition of the author's *Behind the Third Gospel*, I undertook to edit the manuscript and prepare it for publication. I regret that owing to a variety of circumstances, including some other urgent commitments, this task has taken longer than I had originally hoped. I am most grateful to Professor Matthew Black, the Editor of *New Testament Studies*, for his readiness to publish the work in the Monograph Series of the Society for New Testament Studies, and to both Professor Black and his Associate Editor, Professor R. McL. Wilson, for their patient co-operation and many helpful suggestions.

In substance the work has been left in the form in which Dr Taylor left it. Attention has been drawn in the Editorial Notes on pp. 27–30 and 37f., and in occasional additional footnotes marked [Ed.], to subsequent discussions, or discussions which Dr Taylor appeared to have missed. Apart from these additions the editor's work has been limited to checking references and the general revision and tidying up of the manuscript.

It has been a sad privilege to perform this last service for one to whom, as teacher and friend and constant encourager, I owe an incalculable debt. In the course of it I have been reminded continually of the methodical industry and meticulous thoroughness that marked all Dr Taylor's work. Whatever may be the ultimate fate of the Proto-Luke hypothesis of which, as the present work reveals, he remained to the end so staunch a champion, one may dare to hope that this study of the Lukan Passion narrative will be of interest and value to all who are concerned with questions of literary and historical criticism.

Bangor, October 1970   OWEN E. EVANS

xi

ABBREVIATIONS

BC	*The Beginnings of Christianity* (Kirsopp Lake and F. J. Foakes Jackson)
BTG	*Behind the Third Gospel* (V. Taylor)
ET	*The Expository Times*
FG	*The Four Gospels* (B. H. Streeter)
GHD	*The Gospels as Historical Documents* (V. H. Stanton)
JBL	*The Journal of Biblical Literature*
JTS	*The Journal of Theological Studies*
HTFG	*Historical Tradition in the Fourth Gospel* (C. H. Dodd)
IB	*The Interpreter's Bible*
LS	*Die lukanische Sonderquelle* (F. Rehkopf)
NEB	*The New English Bible*
NTS	*New Testament Studies*
RSV	*Revised Standard Version*
SJ	*The Sayings of Jesus* (T. W. Manson)
*	A single asterisk following a list of references means that every occurrence in the particular book or author concerned has been given.
**	A double asterisk means that every occurrence in the entire New Testament has been given.

xii

PART ONE
INTRODUCTION

I. SUMMARY OF CRITICAL OPINION

Before examining the Passion narrative of Lk. xxii–xxiv it is desirable to give some account of earlier research in this field. A useful summary of critical opinion is supplied by J. Moffatt in his *Introduction to the Literature of the New Testament* (3rd ed. 1918)[1] with special attention to the three-source theories of P. Feine, G. H. Müller, B. Weiss, and J. Weiss. A fuller account is given by W. Bussmann in *Synoptische Studien* (1925–31).[2] Bussmann lists the contributions of H. J. Holtzmann, C. Weizsäcker, H. H. Wendt, P. Ewald, P. Feine, J. C. Hawkins, P. Wernle, J. Wellhausen, J. Weiss, B. Weiss, G. H. Müller, A. Jülicher, F. Spitta, K. L. Schmidt, R. Bultmann, Ed. Meyer, E. Burton, B. H. Streeter, and W. Larfeld. The third source is usually designated by the symbol S or, by British scholars, L. As described by the earlier of these writers, S consists of Lukan tradition included in Q, but in the opinion of most of them it is a special source, oral or written, which the evangelist combined with Q. It will be seen that the number of scholars who have defended a three-source theory is considerable, especially when we add the contributions of F. C. Burkitt, V. H. Stanton, J. V. Bartlet, and W. Sanday in Great Britain, A. M. Perry, B. S. Easton, B. W. Bacon, and F. C. Grant in America, and J. Jeremias, H. Schürmann, and F. Rehkopf in Germany.

I propose to give some account of the views of Feine, B. Weiss, and J. Weiss, and of the British, American, and German scholars just mentioned.

P. Feine[3] was the first to describe Luke's use of a third source. In the Passion narrative it included Lk. xxii. 14–23, 31–8, 39–46, 47–53, 54–62, 63–71; xxiii. 1–56 and xxiv. 1–53. B. Weiss[4] included xxii. 1–6, 14–23, 31–4 and 39 – xxiv. 51, and

---

[1] Pp. 274–8.   [2] III, 89–96.
[3] *Eine vorkanonische Überlieferung des Lukas* (1891).
[4] *Die Quellen der synoptischen Überlieferung* (1908).

I-2

J. Weiss[1] xxii. 15–19, 21–3 (?), 24–38; xxiii. 6–9, 11f., 27–31, 34, 39–43; xxiv. 13–53. In his *Life of Christ* (1883), B. Weiss made a significant observation when he wrote, 'The supposition is ever suggesting itself, that beside Mark's Gospel there lay before the Evangelist another comprehensive delineation of the whole life of Jesus, even if his assertions regarding the many men, to whose attempts he refers, will scarcely permit of all the materials peculiar to himself being allotted to this source.'[2]

In Great Britain an important step was taken by F. C. Burkitt in his *Gospel History and its Transmission* (1906) when he claimed that in Luke the source Q contained a story of the Passion. In this form his suggestion has been widely rejected, and rightly, for it leaves unexplained the neglect of the presumed Passion narrative by Matthew. But this rejection tended to obscure the value of his strong case for the independence and historical value of the Lukan Passion narrative.

Burkitt points out that, while the narrative in Matthew is based on Mark, the position is very different in Luke. The third evangelist, he claims, deserts Mark 'to follow another story of the last scenes'.[3] Burkitt lays stress on the saying about 'twelve thrones' in Lk. xxii. 30. He contrasts it with the parallel saying in Mt. xix. 28, where it is inserted into the framework of Mark, and argues that, since Luke does not as a rule disturb the order of his sources, the Lukan saying is a fragment of Q, and that Q contained a story of the Passion as well as discourses. Other narrative matter stood in Q (e.g. the story of the centurion's servant), and there is nothing therefore to surprise one that it should have given an account of the last scenes.[4]

Burkitt supports his suggestion, the speculative character of which he realises, by pointing out the intrinsic merits of the Lukan Passion narrative. In several respects Mark and Luke do not agree as to the time and order in which events occurred, and the superior tradition is that of Luke. These incidents include Peter's denial, the trial by the priests, and the mocking. 'According to Mark', Burkitt writes,

the chief priests try Jesus in the dead of night, and the rough horse-play and buffeting appears to be done by some members of the Council them-

---

[1] *Die Schriften des Neuen Testaments* (1906).　　　[2] *Life of Christ*, I, 80.
[3] *Gospel History and its Transmission*, p. 130.
[4] *Op. cit.* p. 135.

selves while they are waiting till it is time to go to Pilate, not by the Temple guards waiting till it is time for the Council to assemble. I venture to think that S. Luke's account is the more probable.[1]

Similarly, Burkitt maintains the superiority of Luke's account of the mock adoration of Jesus as king by Herod's soldiers, as compared with Mark's story (xv. 16–20a) which ascribes this act to the soldiers of the Roman governor. He points to the 'genuinely Jewish phrase', χριστὸν βασιλέα (= Malka Meshiha, 'King Messiah') in the accusation of the priests before Pilate. Speaking of the words about buying swords (Lk. xxii. 36) he says, 'They are among the saddest words in the Gospels, and the mournful irony with which they are pervaded seems to me wholly alien from the kind of utterance which a Christian Evangelist would invent for his Master.'[2]

Burkitt's contention that the Lukan Passion narrative rests upon an early and valuable source, which is independent of Mark, has great force. The opinion that the source is Q is among the things that pass. The conjunction of the view that the Passion narrative comes from Q undoubtedly delayed the discussion of his main contention. Thus, it is interesting to note that V. H. Stanton's criticism of Burkitt's theory turns exclusively upon the question of Q; it ignores his argument regarding the Lukan Passion narrative.

V. H. Stanton took up the question of Luke's sources in the second volume of his great work, *The Gospels as Historical Documents* (1909). He held that the birth stories and the genealogy were parts of a written source, and maintained that for his account of the ministry of Jesus, Luke used in addition to Mark 'one other principal source', an expanded form of Q. With this source as a foundation a good deal of other material was embodied somewhere in Palestine; 'it has supplied the greater part of the non-Markan matter in the Gospel from the beginning of the Synoptic outline onwards', mainly in two portions, Lk. vi. 17 – viii. 3 and ix. 51 – xviii. 14. He ascribes this source to a writer other than Luke. He draws attention to the temporal connexions between successive paragraphs (xi. 27, 37, 53; xii. 1, 13; xiii. 1, 31; xvi. 14) and concludes that they 'were found by the evangelist in his source, not invented

---

[1] *Op. cit.* pp. 137f.   [2] *Op. cit.* pp. 140f.

by him'.[1] In particular, the accounts of incidents in the history of the Passion and appearances of the risen Christ, peculiar to this Gospel, were added by him. In the Gospel as a whole Stanton notes nine sections whose literary form should in all probability be attributed to the evangelist (v. 1–11; vii. 36–50; viii. 1–3; x. 29–37; xvii. 11–19; xix. 41–4; xxiii. 5–12, 14, 15; xxiii. 39–43; and xxiv).[2]

In his essay in *Oxford Studies in the Synoptic Problem* (1911), 'St Luke's Use of St Mark's Gospel', J. C. Hawkins says that he used to think the strongest arguments in favour of the three-document theories of Feine and others were to be found in Luke's Passion narrative. But closer investigation, he says, led him to think that Luke's additions 'suggest a long and gradual conflation in the mind rather than a simple conflation by the pen'.[3] Luke was a fellow worker with Paul, and so will have been a preacher of the Pauline type. In his preaching the crucifixion would be thrown into special prominence, and this would have its effect when Luke approached this theme in his Gospel. 'May it not have been that the preacher (and perhaps catechist) who afterwards became the Third Evangelist, had for his homiletic purposes gradually supplemented, and in supplementing had to some extent modified and transposed, the generally accepted Markan record, so far as it related to the Passion and Crucifixion?'[4] In this way Hawkins explains the phenomena of Lk. xxii. 14 ff. as due to Luke's 'memories of his past teaching'.

Luke's use of Mark does not favour this view. In *Oxford Studies* W. Sanday expressed a personal preference for Hawkins's earlier view.[5] He pointed out that none of Luke's additions has any doctrinal significance. 'St Luke's additions', he wrote, 'are narrative for narrative's sake, not narrative for the sake of doctrine.'[6] The character of the added matter was naturally accounted for if Luke had access to some special source of information; 'they do not seem to deal with the special doctrinal teaching of St Paul'.[7] This effective criticism tells strongly against Hawkins's suggestion and favours the view that the special Lukan source was a document.

---

[1] *GHD*, II, 229. [2] *Op. cit.* p. 310.
[3] *Oxford Studies in the Synoptic Problem*, p. 90.
[4] *Op. cit.* p. 92. [5] *Op. cit.* p. xiii.
[6] *Op. cit.* p. xiv. [7] *Op. cit.* p. xiv.

In *Oxford Studies* J. C. Hawkins also notes a change in Luke's procedure at ix. 51 and suggests that its cause is due to 'his ceasing to use the Markan document as the framework into which his various extracts were inserted'. He makes two conjectures which may account for this change of procedure. (1) 'Luke may have drawn up this "travel-document" with some special purpose before he knew of, or at least before he began to found a Gospel upon, the Markan *Grundschrift*, and he may thus have had it ready to his hand for incorporation here'.[1] (2) Mark is laid aside possibly because 'at Caesarea or Jerusalem (Acts xxi. 8ff., 15ff.) or elsewhere, a more exact and chronological account of this final journey had been supplied to him by one who had at the time of the commencement of that journey become "an eyewitness and minister of the Word"'.[2] There Hawkins was content to leave the matter, but the question could not long be delayed whether, with due regard to the scientific caution Hawkins enjoined, evidence might be found to warrant a further step.

It is interesting to recall that in another essay in *Oxford Studies*, on Luke's sources, such a step was taken by J. V. Bartlet.[3] He suggests that, in addition to an oral version of Q which he calls QL, Luke used a second written source 'alongside and indeed in preference to Mark'. This source he distinguishes by the symbol S, and he suggests that it was probably written down while Luke was in Caesarea along with Paul. We need not stay to describe more fully the details of Bartlet's hypothesis or the objections to which it is exposed. The objections concern the large extent of S, the suggestion of an oral version of Q, the fact that his hypothesis reduces Luke's part in the composition of his Gospel to a minimum, and the manner in which S is related to Mark. In the introduction to *Oxford Studies*, W. Sanday[4] cordially welcomed Bartlet's views regarding Luke's special source, but he questioned the idea of Q as an oral source and the suggestion that S contained much of the material generally assigned to Q. His closing sentence is so full of significance for our investigation that it must be given in full: 'But I should like to ask whether it is not possible to rally round the clear and sharply drawn definition of Q as it is

---

[1] *Op. cit.* pp. 55f.   [2] *Op. cit.* p. 57.
[3] *Op. cit.* pp. 315–62.   [4] *Op. cit.* pp. xx–xxiii.

presented to us in the earlier essays, and so pass on to the closer testing of the supplementary hypothesis of St Luke's special source.'[1] These are prophetic words, when we remember that B. H. Streeter, the author of some of the essays to which Sanday refers, has taken the very step described. Without departing in any essential particular from the two-document hypothesis, Streeter has passed on 'to the closer testing of the supplementary hypothesis of St Luke's special source', and has found reason to include it in a comprehensive view of the origin of the Third Gospel.

Before discussing Streeter's contribution, consideration must be given to A. M. Perry's *Sources of Luke's Passion Narrative* (1920), which he describes as the most thorough attempt he knows to unravel Luke's sources.[2]

After a detailed examination of the Passion narrative in Luke, Perry concludes that it has been taken from a non-Markan source, which he designates as J or the Jerusalem source, a Greek document, probably translated from Aramaic, which, he conjectures, was produced in the community at Jerusalem about A.D. 45 by a disciple of Jesus. Following E. D. Burton, Perry substitutes for Q two non-Markan sources, one embodied in the Lukan account of the Galilean ministry (G) and the other (P) in the 'Perean' section, and to these J was added. He holds, however, that his results are equally available for those who accept the two-document hypothesis,[3] and this is largely true. The date and other details in Perry's construction are open to question, but the non-Markan character of J and its considerable historical value are of permanent value. Like Burkitt, Perry holds that in many of its peculiar features 'the narrative is inherently more probable' than Mark 'in its details and relation'.[4] In many respects it anticipates Streeter's findings, and to these we now turn.

Streeter's Proto-Luke hypothesis is well known and it is not necessary to describe it in detail, especially as our main interest in this investigation is the Passion narrative. Stated in its simplest terms, it is the claim that Luke first combined Q and his special source L about A.D. 60, and some twenty years later

---

[1] *Op. cit.* p. xxiii.   [2] *The Four Gospels*, p. 217n.
[3] The latter appears to be the more probable alternative.
[4] *Sources of Luke's Passion Narrative*, p. 99.

expanded Q + L in compiling his Gospel.[1] The Lukan Passion narrative, he maintains, was composed by Luke, and contains extracts from Mark in xxii. 18, 22, 42, 46f., 52–61, 71; xxiii. 3, 22, 25f., 33–4b, 38, 44–6, 52f., and xxiv. 6, with possible assimilations to Mark in xxii. 69; xxiii. 35, 49, 51; xxiv. 1–3, 9f.[2] Whether these passages are inserted from Mark or are assimilated to it are among the questions to be examined afresh in the present investigation. It will be recalled that where Mark and Proto-Luke are parallel, Streeter suggested that Proto-Luke is sometimes inferior in historical value and sometimes superior, and that 'as historical authorities they should probably be regarded as on the whole of approximately equal value'.[3] At its inception his hypothesis was received with considerable favour in Great Britain and America.

In a full review of *Behind the Third Gospel*, A. S. Peake observed that, 'Even if at all points the author's suggestions may not ultimately be accepted, a substantial part of his conclusions will probably commend themselves to his fellow-workers.'[4] H. G. Wood wrote, 'This theory is certainly attractive, and I should say that a high degree of probability attaches to it.'[5] G. S. Duncan declared that Proto-Luke was no longer a hypothesis; it was an established fact and the unearthing of it meant the discovery of what is 'our earliest Gospel'.[6] C. H. Dodd said that in his opinion Streeter's hypothesis is right in substance, and that behind the Third Gospel probably lies a 'proto-Luke' which might be as early as Mark, but he doubted whether we are entitled to give the same weight to this hypothetical document as we give to the Second Gospel. His reasons for hesitation were: (a) 'We do not know what amount of revision "proto-Luke" underwent in being incorporated in the Third Gospel', and (b) 'The peculiarly Lucan material, on its merits, seems in places almost demonstrably secondary to Mark, even though in some places it may be thought to have preserved a more primitive tradition.'[7] T. W. Manson wrote, 'It is probable that

[1] Cf. *BTG*, pp. 182–215.   [2] Cf. *FG*, p. 222.
[3] *FG*, p. 222.
[4] *The Holborn Review* (July 1926), pp. 368–70.
[5] *The Friend* (July 1926).
[6] *The Review of the Churches* (July 1926).
[7] *The Parables of the Kingdom* (1935), p. 40.

the first stage in the composition [of Luke] was the bringing together of Q and L to form a document about the size of Mark.' 'Later, material from Mark was added and the Birth and Infancy narratives were prefixed to produce the Gospel as we know it.'[1] This, of course, is the Proto-Luke hypothesis.

It is sometimes said by way of reproach that the hypothesis has received much less support in Germany and America than in Great Britain. This is true; but in Germany, as will be seen later,[2] J. Jeremias, H. Schürmann, and F. Rehkopf have added their support to the hypothesis. American opinion was divided, but favourable judgements were expressed by such leading scholars as B. S. Easton, F. C. Grant, and B. W. Bacon, in addition to A. M. Perry, already mentioned.

Easton's commentary on Luke (1926) appeared too early to take full account of the new theory. All the more interesting, therefore, are many opinions and judgements in the commentary which are in agreement with it. In addition to the two-document hypothesis, Easton gave an important place to the use of the L source by Luke, assigning over 500 verses to this document.[3] He accepted the view that the evangelist inserted Lk. vi. 20 – viii. 3 and Lk. ix. 51 – xviii. 14 into Mark's narrative and observed that after Mk. xii, 'Luke's narrative is generally based on a non-Markan source'. Of the historical value of L he wrote,

It contains much matter of high worth, especially in the Passion narrative, but it contains also matter that is certainly secondary, with versions of historic scenes that betray theological or apologetic interests. Broadly speaking, the L narrative sections stand perhaps halfway between the best Markan tradition and the versions in the Fourth Gospel. But in the transmission of Christ's sayings the case is decidedly better, and in many respects L's contributions (particularly as regards parables) are inestimable.[4]

In the commentary from xxii. 14 onwards, the L tradition is held to be basic.

F. C. Grant in *The Growth of the Gospels* (1933) expressed a strong conviction of the fundamental correctness of Streeter's hypothesis. 'An examination of the reconstructed Proto-Luke',

---

[1] *A Companion to the Bible* (1939), p. 116. So also W. Manson, H. Balmforth, and H. K. Luce in their Commentaries on Luke (1930–3).

[2] See pp. 17–21. [3] *Commentary*, p. xxviii.

[4] *Op. cit.* p. xxviii.

he wrote, 'will probably convince most readers that this was a real, if not wholly comprehensive, "Gospel", on a par with St Mark, and often as a source to be preferred to Mark, though they sometimes confirm each other.'[1] Especially in the Passion section, he affirmed, the narrative of Proto-Luke was in some particulars preferable to the other Gospels, preferable even to Luke which had not added greatly to the value of the narrative by the incorporation of the Markan account of the last scenes. 'I cannot believe', he wrote, 'that in the following passages, for example, the Marcan element is the kernel or structural basis: xi. 15–18; xiv. 34; xvii. 2, 31; xix. 45f.; xxii. 3–6, 18–19, 25f., 34; xxiii. 3, 26, 38, 44f. It seems almost obvious that Marcan material has been inserted into a Q plus L framework.'[2] Later, in *The Gospels: Their Origin and Their Growth* (1957), influenced by Creed's criticism of Streeter's hypothesis, he spoke with greater reserve and indeed with considerable hesitation.[3]

B. W. Bacon's references to Proto-Luke in *Studies in Matthew* (1930) are brief and characteristically incisive. He pointed out that Streeter's views 'advance but little those published by Paul Feine...(1891) and since that date accepted (so far as the doctrine of a "Proto-Luke" is concerned) by many of our leading German and English critics'.[4] 'Great impetus', he wrote, 'has undoubtedly been given by Streeter's advocacy to the theory of L (accepted since 1900 by the present writer; cf. *An Introduction to the New Testament*, NewYork, 1900, pp. 214ff.)'.[5] Of Streeter's confession that for many years he was a victim to the illusion that Matthew and Luke used no other documents, or at least, none of anything like the same value as Mark and Q, he added, 'Others may decline with thanks to be included in this confession.'

It will be seen that at first the Proto-Luke hypothesis was received with considerable favour in Great Britain and America. Subsequently, however, it lost ground under the criticisms of J. W. Hunkin, J. M. Creed, and R. H. Lightfoot, and their objections must now be considered.

[1] *The Growth of the Gospels*, p. 170.
[2] *Op. cit.* p. 172n.
[3] *The Gospels : Their Origin and Their Growth*, pp. 27, 118f., 129ff.
[4] *Studies in Matthew*, p. 505.   [5] *Ibid.*

2. OBJECTIONS

Objections to the existence of a special Passion source used by Luke have been made by various scholars, notably by J. W. Hunkin[1] and J. M. Creed[2] in Great Britain and by S. MacLean Gilmour[3] in America, and some account of their arguments must now be given.

Both Hunkin and Creed conceded that before he wrote his Gospel Luke had already combined the sayings-source Q with his special tradition L. Hunkin was ready to accept Streeter's hypothesis so far as it concerned Lk. ix. 51 – xviii. 14, 'the most considerable block of material', he says, 'from Q+L', and suggested that Q, worked over and improved upon by the evangelist, entered into the final composition only through the document Q+L. 'The theory', he wrote, 'that this collection was formed by building on to extracts from Q material collected by St Luke during his visit to Palestine, particularly during his stay at Caesarea, is an illuminating theory which seems to fit the main facts and may well be accepted.' Creed wrote in similar terms. To his submission that Mark must be regarded as 'a determining factor' in the construction of Luke from the outset, he added, 'This, however, is not necessarily inconsistent with the hypothesis that Q and some of Luke's peculiar material may have been already combined and may have lain before Luke as a single document.'[4]

Both Hunkin and Creed contend that the Lukan Passion narrative is a revised edition of Mark's account. Material from Q+L has been fitted into the Markan framework. In *The New Testament: A Conspectus* (1950), Hunkin reaffirms this view and describes it as 'a modification of the theory of Streeter and Vincent Taylor'.[5]

Creed's main criticisms are put forward in an important footnote in his commentary on Luke.[6] It may be doubted if any footnote in works on Synoptic criticism has exerted so much

---

[1] *JTS*, xxviii (April 1927), 250–62; *The New Testament: A Conspectus* (1950), p. 78.
[2] *St Luke*, pp. l, lviiin., lxiv, 86, 140, 262.
[3] *JBL*, lxvii (1948), 143–52; *IB*, viii, 16–18.   [4] *St Luke*, p. lviiin.
[5] *The New Testament: A Conspectus*, p. 78.
[6] *St Luke*, p. lviiin.

influence. Many critics[1] have based their rejection of the Proto-Luke hypothesis on this footnote. It is therefore necessary to examine it carefully.

Creed argues that 'the subtraction of Markan material (in Luke) leaves an amorphous collection of narrative and discourse, the greater part of which is thrown without intelligible reason into the unsuitable form of a "travel document" (Lk. ix. 52 – xviii)'. Moreover, signs of the use of Mark are clear in Lk. iii. 3 and 16, and above all in the Passion narrative. In the Passion narrative not only are there complete sections which are unmistakably taken from Mark (e.g. Lk. xxii. 7–13, 54–61), but Markan phrases appear in the middle of sections which in other respects differ considerably from Mark (e.g. xxii. 19a, 22, 47, 52, 71; xxiii. 3). If Luke already possessed a full and independent non-Markan narrative, he argues, 'it seems unlikely that afterwards he would have interpolated occasional sentences and verses from Mark'. Streeter's reply to these arguments,[2] I think, has not received the attention it deserves. To the objection that Proto-Luke is 'an amorphous collection of narrative and discourse', he points out that it could not well be anything else than amorphous, since the compiler did not enjoy the advantage of Mark through his association with Peter. 'What the historian has to explain', he says, 'in a community of Jewish origin, is not the existence of amorphous collections – which was the normal thing – but the emergence of a non-amorphous biography like Mark.' The statement that Luke would not have interpolated occasional verses into a non-Markan Passion narrative is effectively answered by the American scholar, A. M. Perry, who writes, 'I must beg leave to differ: not only is this, in essence, what Luke in his preface professes to have done, but it is exactly what any one who rejects the Proto-Luke hypothesis has to assume that he *has* done with Mark, surely "a full and independent narrative".'[3] These replies are conclusive, but on the other hand the same

[1] See, for example, E. C. Hoskyns and F. N. Davey, *The Riddle of the New Testament*, p. 104.
[2] In the Preface to the fourth impression of *FG*.
[3] In an article on 'Luke's Disputed Passion-Source', *ET*, XLVI, 259. The same point is made in my *Formation of the Gospel Tradition*, Appendix A, pp. 194f.: 'Surely, if Luke had written an independent narrative of the Passion, and then later found new and interesting information in Mark's

cannot be said of answers to Creed's claim that Mark is a determining factor in the composition of Luke. Supporters of the Proto-Luke hypothesis have not done justice to this objection, doubtless from the fear of making damaging concessions, and this is to be regretted because its admission is by no means necessarily fatal to the hypothesis.[1]

In addition to comments on narratives in Lk. xxii. 14 – xxiv. 11 in the Commentary, Creed defended his conclusions in an important article in *The Expository Times*.[2] In this essay he agrees that the Passion narrative is crucial to the defence of the hypothesis. Examining the list of passages claimed by Streeter and myself as 'insertions' into Luke's account, he says there is only one passage, Lk. xxii. 19a, where there is an attractive case for this explanation.

Creed agrees that Luke follows his Markan source far less closely in the Passion narrative than in the body of his Gospel and argues that we have no right to assume that he will always treat his Markan source in the same way. He cites the opinion of Hunkin that in the eschatological discourse of Lk. xxi the proportion of non-Markan words rises far above the average level. This argument is not convincing. First put forward by F. C. Burkitt,[3] it is not sustained by a close examination of Lk. xxi. 5–19, where the percentage of Markan words is relatively high, and still less by Lk. xxi. 20–36, where apart from vv. 21a, 23a, 26b–27, and 29–33, the percentage in the rest of vv. 20–36, a manifest literary unity, is no more than 10.6 per cent.[4]

Creed's objection to the view that several Markan passages are 'insertions' in Luke's Passion narrative is no more satisfactory. He concedes that other passages besides Lk. xxii. 19a might be so regarded if the rest of the evidence favoured this view. As examples he mentions Lk. xxiii. 26, 34b, 44f., but rejects the need to explain Lk. xxii. 47, 50, 52f., 71; xxiii. 3 as

---

Gospel, it would be the most natural thing in the world to insert extracts from such an authority into his own story. Not to do so would be inconsistent with the claims of his Preface.'

[1] See below, p. 33.
[2] *ET*, XLVI, 101–7: 'L and the Structure of the Lucan Gospel.'
[3] *BC*, II, 106ff.
[4] See *BTG*, pp. 101ff., and below, pp. 31f.

Markan 'enrichments' of Luke's narrative. An examination of these and other passages does not, I believe, sustain this rejection.[1] This is especially true in the case of Lk. xxiii. 3. Here, out of nineteen words, sixteen are common to Luke and Mark, ten of them in close succession, while the rest of the narrative (vv. 1f. and 4f.) has only five words in common with Mark, in the two phrases ὁ Πειλᾶτος and ὁ δὲ Πειλᾶτος.[2]

Another strong opponent of the Proto-Luke hypothesis is R. H. Lightfoot, who after describing it as 'misleading and unnecessary'[3] and 'extremely doubtful'[4] replaced the latter phrase by the observation that it is 'less widely accepted on the Continent and in America than in this country'.[5] A. Farrer went further, and spoke of it as 'a theory which still has adherents' and as 'incapable of reasonable defence'.[6] A. R. C. Leaney, in his *Commentary on Luke* (1958), expresses strong conviction as to its unsoundness, but without advancing any argument in support of this conclusion beyond the opinion that its lack of either an apocalypse or a Passion narrative would deprive 'Proto-Luke' of all claim to be called a gospel.[7]

It is to be regretted that these scholars have not indicated the arguments which have led them to draw such trenchant conclusions. Their rejection is manifest, but not their grounds of objection. W. F. Howard wrote, 'It seems to me that the main arguments of Streeter and his henchman, Dr. Vincent Taylor, have never been successfully refuted.'[8] And C. S. C. Williams has declared that suspicion and dislike of the theory of Proto-Luke have led to more abuse than argument against it. It is a reasonable and justifiable assumption and a possible view, he says, that the Third Gospel consists of Q + L, a Lukan Passion narrative, the birth stories, and Mark. 'Like the theory of the existence of Q, the Proto-Lukan theory survives, and premature announcements of their demise are "greatly exaggerated".'[9]

---

[1] See my article in *ET*, xlvi, 236–8, and Creed's rejoinder, *ET*, xlvi, 378f.
[2] *BTG*, pp. 52f.
[3] *History and Interpretation in the Gospels* (1935), p. 164.
[4] *ET*, liii, 51.
[5] *The Gospel Message of St Mark* (1950), p. 99.
[6] *A Study in Mark*, p. 210.   [7] *St Luke*, p. 33.
[8] *The London Quarterly and Holborn Review* (Jan. 1952), p. 11.
[9] *Peake's Commentary on the Bible*, revised ed., para. 655c.

Lastly, reference may be made to the objections of S. MacLean Gilmour. In an article in the *Journal of Biblical Literature*,[1] afterwards embodied in his commentary on *Luke*,[2] Gilmour says that he wishes to criticise the hypothesis 'that Q+L amounted to a complete gospel and that it provided Luke with the framework of his final draft'. Of these criticisms the first is beside the point. Streeter does not claim that Proto-Luke actually amounted to 'a complete gospel'; the furthest he goes is to refer to it as 'something very like a complete gospel', 'practically a gospel', 'a kind of half-way house' to a gospel.[3] For myself, I have maintained that it is 'like the first draft of a great work'.[4] Gilmour's second objection is more detailed. He claims that Lk. iii. 1 – iv. 30 is not a continuous block of non-Markan matter, since at crucial points Luke betrays unmistakable dependence on Mark, and that his use of Mark and his other sources in Lk. xxii. 14 – xxiv is comparable with that of Lk. iii. 1 – iv. 30. In the Passion narrative he lists passages which constitute a special tradition. These amount to ninety-five verses[5] out of 180, that is, more than half. Most of this material, he contends, appears to be Luke's own composition based on oral tradition. Luke seems to have employed a special documentary tradition of the Last Supper, but the Markan verses 19*a* and 22 are still a base for it. In Lk. xxii. 24–6 we have to do with some independent tradition, but it is parallel to Mk. x. 42–5 and the opening verse is editorial. So too Lk. xxii. 31–3 is Luke's composition, but in verse 34 it concludes with material drawn from Mk. xiv. 30. The account of Jesus's prayer of petition, and those of the betrayal, arrest and Peter's denial are all based on Mark. So also xxiii. 3, 26, and the account of the crucifixion are wholly Markan in origin, also xxiii. 44–7, the list of witnesses in xxiii. 49, the story of the burial and that of the empty tomb. Lk. xxiv. 6*b*–11 is an editorial addition, and v. 10*a* appears to be dependent on Mk. xvi. 1. It is clear, Gilmour says, that Luke was able to draw on a variety of traditions with which to amplify and recast Mark, but his basic dependence on Mark's account is equally clear. So he draws the triumphant conclusion that the Proto-Luke hypothesis, while not necessarily a 'snare and a delusion', falls short of demon-

---

[1] *JBL*, LXVII (1948), 143–52.   [2] *IB*, VIII, 3–434.
[3] *FG*, pp. 207, 214, 217.   [4] *BTG*, p. 212.
[5] In the Commentary it is reduced to forty-eight verses.

stration and should be abandoned as a brilliant but not convincing vagary of criticism. In all this we miss a detailed investigation and a linguistic argument which ought to have been pursued before the article was embodied in the Commentary. Here the phrase 'a snare and a delusion' is replaced by the more modest claim that the hypothesis 'may be dismissed'.[1]

3. RECENT DEVELOPMENTS

The opinion that a special source lies behind Lk. xxii. 14 – xxiv has long been held by many German scholars and in recent years has been supported by J. Jeremias, H. Schürmann, and F. Rehkopf in connexion with the Proto-Luke hypothesis as a whole.

The views of Jeremias are put forward in the third edition of his *Die Abendmahlsworte Jesu* (1960), translated into English in *The Eucharistic Words of Jesus* (1966). In discussing Luke's account of the Last Supper he says, 'The *Lukan* account... (xxii. 7–39) follows Luke's special source from v. 14 onwards.'[2] 'Whenever Luke follows the Markan narrative in his own gospel he follows painstakingly the Markan order, pericope for pericope. Up to the passion narrative there are only two insignificant deviations, Lk. vi. 17–19; viii. 19–21...Luke was therefore, in contrast to Matthew, an enemy of rearrangement.'[3] He concludes that 'deviations in the order of the material must therefore be regarded as indications that Luke is not following Mark'.[4] He points out that in Luke's account of the Last Supper there is a large number of such deviations; the eschatological saying precedes the words of institution (Lk. xxii. 15–18), the announcement of the betrayal follows them (xxii. 21–3); the lament over the traitor precedes the speculations of the disciples (xxii. 22); the prophecy of the denial is made before the departure to Gethsemane (xxii. 33f.). Thus, Luke's report from xxii. 14 onwards 'is no longer built upon a Markan basis, but comes from *Urlukas*'.[5] Only xxii. 7–13 still belongs to the Markan material. In a footnote he adds, 'It is my opinion that Luke has incorporated the

---

[1] *IB*, viii, 18.
[2] *The Eucharistic Words of Jesus*, p. 97.
[3] *Op. cit.* p. 98.   [4] *Ibid.*
[5] *Op. cit.* p. 99.

Markan material into his own and not *vice versa*.' In his article
'Perikopen-Umstellungen bei Lukas?',[1] Jeremias agrees that
Luke transposes words within a sentence or section or from one
section to another, but rejects the view that he transposes
sections.

In a table Jeremias sets out the non-Markan and the Markan
sections very much as Streeter does in *The Four Gospels*, accepting
the non-Markan character of Lk. vi. 12–16 (the choice of the
Twelve) in which both sources coincided. At this point the
evangelist introduced his special material, transposing Lk. vi.
17–19 (many miracles of healing) to form the introduction to the
Lukan Sermon. The only other transposition is Lk. viii. 19–21
(the visit of the family of Jesus), which he places in the first
suitable place in the Markan section Lk. viii. 4 – ix. 50. In the
opinion of Jeremias, a completely different state of affairs exists
in the Passion narrative of Luke. In chapter xxii alone, he points
out, there are six alterations of order in narratives as compared
with Mark. Further, a comparison of the narrative of the
crucifixion (Lk. xxiii. 26–49) with Mk. xv. 20*b*–41 shows that if
Luke followed Mark, he has completely mixed up (*vollständig
durcheinandergewirbelt*) the material. He concludes that in Lk. xxii.
14ff. a new block of material begins in which Luke follows his
special tradition.

Closely similar results have been reached by H. Schürmann
and F. Rehkopf, to both of whom Jeremias refers. Schürmann's
source-critical investigation of Lk. xxii. 7–38, *Quellenkritische
Untersuchung des lukanischen Abendmahlsberichtes Lk. xxii. 7–38*
(1953–7), is a very considerable work of 436 pages (with 1465
detailed footnotes), in three parts.[2] While not neglecting numerical considerations, in the presence of 'common' words, his main
interest is in questions of vocabulary, constructions, and style.
These are examined and compared with those of Mark in
exhaustive detail, even more fully than in the works of Hawkins
and Cadbury. Although the investigation is limited to 32 verses,
his results enable Schürmann to suggest important opinions on

---

[1] *NTS*, IV (Jan. 1958), 115–19, in reply to H. F. D. Sparks in his article
in *NTS*, III (May 1957), 'St Luke's Transpositions', 219–23.

[2] Part I, *Der Paschamahlbericht Lk. xxii. (7–14), 15–18* (1953); Part II, *Der
Einsetzungsbericht Lk. xxii. 19–20* (1955); Part III, *Jesu Abschiedsrede Lk.
xxii. 21–38* (1957).

the special Lukan source as a whole, including the Passion narrative. He suggests that xxii. 14, 20*b*, 21–3 and 33f. were taken from Mark, but that 15–20*a*, 24–32 and 35–8 were derived from a pre-Lukan source.[1] He further maintains that xxii. 7–13 and 14 are a Lukan version of Mk. xiv. 12–18*a* which Luke used as a suitable introduction to xxii. 15ff. instead of a (presumed) non-Markan preface to his pre-Lukan account of the Last Supper.[2]

There is much in these suggestions which calls for further discussion. Meantime it may be noted that he assigns the greater part of Lk. xxii. 14–38, amounting to eighteen and a half verses out of twenty-five, to the special source. If, as many have maintained,[3] verses 14, 21, 23, and 33 are also non-Markan, the Markan element is reduced to verses 20*b*, 22 and 34. A special problem is raised by the longer text in xxii. 19*b*–20 which, apart from 20*b*, Schürmann includes in the pre-Lukan source.[4] A renewed interest in the textual problem is illustrated by the fact that F. G. Kenyon, S. C. E. Legg, C. S. C. Williams,[5] and many continental scholars accept this passage as a genuine part of the Lukan text.

F. Rehkopf's *Die lukanische Sonderquelle* (1959) is wider in scope than Schürmann's investigation since it treats broadly the pre-Lukan source in the Third Gospel as a whole, but is more restricted in range since it examines in detail only two narratives in the Passion narrative, Lk. xxii. 21–3 (the prophecy of the betrayal) and xxii. 47–53 (the arrest). He defends this choice of narratives by the claim that at an earlier stage the Passion narrative began with the arrest of Jesus.[6] In support of this view he cites the opinions of Jeremias[7] and Bultmann,[8] in particular the arguments of Jeremias (1) that in John the order of the Passion narrative agrees with the Synoptic accounts from the arrest onwards, (2) that in Mk. ix. 31 and x. 33 the prophecies of the Passion begin with the delivering up of Jesus, and (3) that in

---

[1] *Jesu Abschiedsrede*, p. 139. [2] *Der Paschamahlbericht*, pp. 122f.
[3] Cf. V. Taylor, *BTG*, p. 43; P. Winter, *NTS*, II, 207–9; IV, 223–7.
[4] *Der Einsetzungsbericht*. On this see below, pp. 52–6.
[5] Cf. *Alterations to the Text of the Synoptic Gospels and Acts*, pp. 47–51.
[6] *Op. cit.* pp. 5f.
[7] *Die Abendmahlsworte Jesu* (3rd ed. 1960), pp. 88f.; *The Eucharistic Words of Jesus*, pp. 94f.
[8] *Die Geschichte der synoptischen Tradition* (1931), pp. 297–308; *The History of the Synoptic Tradition* (English translation, 1963), pp. 275–84.

Mk. xiv. 43 the traitor is introduced with the words 'Judas one of the Twelve', as if he were still wholly unknown to the reader, although in Mk. xiv. 10 he had already been designated 'Judas Iscariot, who was one of the Twelve'. Rehkopf uses the same literary-critical method adopted by Schürmann. A special feature is that repeatedly he takes into account that of the Synoptic writers Luke has most agreements with the Johannine narrative. This agreement he explains by the claim that both evangelists independently rest upon a common tradition.[1] Most important of all, he supplies a considerable list of words and phrases illustrative of pre-Lukan speech-usage, consisting of seventy-eight items, together with a list of vocatives, cases of the historical present tense, and substitutes for the divine name by the third person plural, all characteristic of the special source.[2] This list is discussed later.[3] In general it may be said that the tendency of Rehkopf's study is to reduce the amount of Markan material in Lk. xxii. 14ff., and thus to assign most of the narrative to the pre-Lukan source. As against Schürmann, he claims that the whole of xxii. 21–3 is pre-Lukan,[4] and he rejects the view that xxii. 14 and 33f. are based on Mark. He recognises a Markan insertion in xxii. 52b–53a, but in addition to xxii. 20b appears to admit the Markan origin only of xxiii. 26.

For several reasons Rehkopf's list of words and phrases illustrative of sources is as yet *sub judice*. It may be objected that too limited an area of Luke is left for comparison when passages claimed as sources are deducted. But against this it must be remembered that Rehkopf supplies the instances in Acts of the words and phrases in question. Since the Gospel and Acts are by the same writer, the material for comparison is in consequence greatly extended. In many cases there are no examples of the words and phrases in Acts and in other cases few only. The list can therefore be used in detecting sources, but it must not be used in a mechanical manner, and in Part Two I have nowhere employed it apart from numerical and critical considerations. Elsewhere I have described the list as 'a key, not a master-key, for use in Synoptic research', and such it is.

[1] Cf. V. Taylor, *BTG*, pp. 221–30; A. M. Perry, *The Sources of Luke's Passion Narrative*; A. Harnack, *Luke the Physician*, pp. 224–31.
[2] *LS*, pp. 91–9.   [3] See pp. 24–7.
[4] *Op. cit.* p. 30.

Rehkopf's conclusions are reminiscent of the Proto-Luke hypothesis. He maintains that L^1 and Q had already been combined before Luke drew upon Mark and the birth stories of Lk. i and ii, and that the latter come from a different source. The special Lukan source amounted to two-thirds of the Gospel, and included Lk. iii. 1 – iv. 30; v. 1–11; vi. 12 – viii. 3 (except vi. 17–19); ix. 51 – xviii. 14; xix. 1–44 (except xix. 29–36); xxi. 34–8; xxii. 14 – xxiv. 53. This is virtually Proto-Luke.

These conclusions of Jeremias, Schürmann, and Rehkopf add weight to the Proto-Luke hypothesis. They rebut the suggestion that it is accepted only in Great Britain and make positive contributions to its acceptance.

In 1954 P. Winter discussed 'The Treatment of His Sources by the Third Evangelist' in an important article in *Studia Theologica*.[2] The treatment concerns Lk. xxi–xxiv, and its special interest is that Winter claims that these chapters are a fusion of Markan and non-Markan material. Luke's sources, he believes, are L (a fusion of a special source S and of Q),[3] Mark and Sx (non-editorial passages later than Mark). In the Passion narrative Winter distinguishes a non-Markan source or sources in Lk. xxii. 14–46, 63–5 and finds a non-Markan undercurrent in many parts of Lk. xxiii. In Lk. xxiv the section vv. 13–53 is non-Markan apart from an editorial supplement in vv. 21*b*–24. In contrast with supporters of the Proto-Luke hypothesis he holds that Lk. xxii. 54*b*–62 (with a residue of non-Markan matter) and Lk. xxiv. 1–11 are based on Mark. Other elements (Lk. xxii. 66*b*–71; xxiii. 27–31 [Sx], 39–43 [Sx]; xxiv. 36–43) contain either post-editorial insertions or haggadic material. How important Winter's studies are may be seen from his conclusions. Thus (1) he thinks that the source used in Lk. xxi–xxiv was a literary record with qualities and characteristics of its own; (2) that the Third Evangelist's devotion to accuracy was

---

[1] It should be explained that Rehkopf's symbol for the special source is S and that he uses L to denote Q+S. He rejects the hypothesis that Luke = Mark + Q + birth stories + matter peculiar to Luke (L). Like Streeter he maintains that Luke = (Q + L) + Mark + birth stories.

[2] VIII, ii (1954), 138–72. See my comment on this article in *ET*, LXVIII, 95.

[3] Winter's use of the symbols S and L agrees with that of Rehkopf. See above, n. 1.

painstaking in the extreme; (3) that the Third Evangelist was not the author of the source. In an important footnote[1] he writes:

There are indications that L was a 'Gospel', that is, a writing that contained an account of Jesus' Passion and Resurrection. The ending of L differed from that of Mark and had no record of the Empty Tomb. If Lk. xxiv. 13–35 is based on L, there may have been an early account of an appearance of the Risen Christ to Peter.

Whether we can distinguish between the work of the evangelist and the author of L, whether post-editorial elements are to be found in Lk. xxii–xxiv, and whether L can be distinguished from S and Sx – these are problems which need to be examined. The basic contention, however, on which Winter is in agreement with the other scholars whose work has been reviewed in this section, is that the Lukan Passion narrative is not merely a re-editing of Mark. 'For this narrative', he writes,[2] 'the Evangelist used *beside* the Marcan account another record, and it appears to me that this non-Marcan record formed a coherent consecutive narrative.'[3]

Among British scholars S. I. Buse, lecturer in New Testament Studies in the University College of North Wales, Bangor, has made a valuable contribution to the study of the Synoptic Passion narratives in two articles in *New Testament Studies*. In the first, 'St John and the Marcan Passion Narrative',[4] Buse points

---

[1] *Op. cit.* p. 139.

[2] See Winter's comment on his own article, in *ET*, LXVIII, 95.

[3] In a review of Schürmann's work (*NTS*, II, 207–9; IV, 223–7) Winter dissents in many matters of detail from the latter's conclusions but adds: 'The differences between the result of Schürmann's analysis and my own tentative probing are differences of detail, based on a different methodological approach, and not differences of principle as regards the question of considering the extant Lucan Passion Narrative to be of composite character.' He describes Schürmann's investigation as 'the most thorough and most detailed style-critical investigation, in any language, of the sources that went into the Lucan description of the Last Supper', and as 'indispensable to anyone who intends to examine the style-critical principles by which the Third Evangelist was guided and his editorial methods in joining together narrative elements and pronouncement stories that were drawn from disparate sources'. 'In this respect', Winter claims, 'the work Schürmann has done on Lk. xxii. 7–38 will assist the pursuit of studies in any part of the Third Gospel' (*op. cit.* IV, 226) [Ed.].

[4] *NTS*, IV (1958), 215ff.

out that John has no parallel to those parts of Mark which I have suggested in my commentary on Mark[1] were derived from a source A close enough to imply dependence, while he has many striking resemblances to a source B, often word-for-word identity of expression. He concludes that the Fourth Evangelist must have been acquainted, not with our Gospel according to St Mark, but with one (or more) of its sources. He suggests that B, including so much that may be Petrine in origin, had an independent existence before Mark incorporated it in his narrative of the last days of our Lord. In the second article, 'St John and the Passion Narratives of St Matthew and St Luke',[2] he argues that the agreements between Matthew and John are neither numerous nor of a decisive character, whereas those between Luke and John in parts at least of the Passion narratives are very close, so much so as to make sheer coincidence a most improbable supposition. 'A justifiable deduction', he says, 'seems to be that Luke knew the Passion narrative parts of which occur in Mark's B stratum.' The most likely explanation of the facts, he maintains, is that John, Luke and Mark were all showing knowledge of the same Passion narrative. 'The deadlock', he adds, 'in the study of the Lucan Passion narrative may be broken by this discovery that some of the so-called Marcan material in Luke came to Mark out of a Passion Source which was known to Luke before he handled the Gospel according to St Mark.'[3] This result is in line with some recent tendencies, as described above, in German research.

A further contribution to the study of the Proto-Luke hypothesis is the commentary on Luke[4] by G. B. Caird, of Mansfield College, Oxford. Caird remints many of the arguments of Streeter in seven considerations including the eleven doublets in Luke and the seventeen cases in which he diverges from the order of Mark in i. 1 – xiv. 11, the twelve transpositions in the Passion narrative, and other arguments, and concludes, 'These seven considerations together may not constitute a proof of the sound-

---

[1] *St Mark*, pp. 649ff.
[2] *NTS*, VII (1960), 65–76. He replies to the criticism of P. Borgen, *NTS*, V (1959), 246ff., that he had taken into account only the agreements of John with Mark and had not considered the similarities with Luke and Matthew.
[3] *Op. cit.* p. 76.
[4] Penguin Books, *Pelican Gospel Commentaries*, edited by D. E. Nineham.

ness of the Proto-Luke theory, but they do reveal the total inadequacy of its rival',[1] and he adopts the theory as a working hypothesis in his commentary. The tide, it would appear, has turned.

DETACHED NOTE ON REHKOPF'S LIST

Rehkopf includes in his list seventy-eight words and four constructions in Luke which he thinks are characteristic of a pre-Lukan source. They include (1) words and phrases rarely or never used by Luke independently, (2) Markan words replaced by Luke predominantly or always, (3) words in contrast to a synonym or similar Lukan expression which he usually prefers, (4) words in the non-Markan sections which are present relatively frequently, and (5) words rarely or never found in the Acts of the Apostles in discourses and the 'We-sections'. He includes in his list words which occur at least three times. The constructions include (1) vocatives, (2) substantives used as vocatives, (3) verbs in the historical present tense, and (4) replacements of the divine name by the third person plural. He uses the symbol L to denote material peculiar to Luke combined with sayings from Q and words from the birth stories. This is different from British usage, where L is used to describe material peculiar to Luke alone. Altogether there are twenty-three words common to the birth stories and L, but of these fifteen would stand in the list apart from the birth stories. Only eight are open to challenge, but seven of these can claim to be included since they are found in Acts once only or never. Αἰνέω has a doubtful claim since it appears in the birth stories twice and in Acts three times, while it stands in L only twice of which one, xxiv. 51, is textually doubtful. Thus, Rehkopf is entitled to claim twenty-two of these words for his list.

Twenty-six words are common to the lists of Hawkins[2] and Rehkopf. The question therefore arises whether these words are characteristic of Luke or whether they belong to the vocabulary of the special Lukan source. Only three do not appear to meet Rehkopf's conditions; they are characteristic of L rather than of

[1] *Op. cit.* p. 27.
[2] 'Words and Phrases Characteristic of St Luke's Gospel', in *Horae Synopticae*[2] (1909).

the Gospel as a whole. In addition to αἰνέω (mentioned already) they include ἀπόστολος (twenty-eight times in Acts) and ἰδοῦ γάρ (in the birth stories three times, in L twice only, and in Acts once). Thus twenty-three are not characteristic of Luke, but belong to Rehkopf's list and are features of pre-Lukan usage. In the Passion narrative there are no less than forty-three words from Rehkopf's list. Among these are αἰνέω, ἀπόστολος and ἰδοῦ γάρ, already questioned, and ἐγγίζω = προσέρχομαι, which may be challenged since it is not certain in how many cases it is the equivalent of προσέρχομαι. In all Rehkopf appears to be justified in including at least seventy-three words and phrases in his list.

Four of these words and phrases call for further comment. πλήν is claimed by Hawkins as characteristic of Luke, but Rehkopf is able to show that it appears only in passages based on sources (Acts (1), Matt. (5), Paul (5), Rev. (1), Luke (14/15) all in L). More striking is the record of εἶπεν *c. dat.* (Acts (7), Luke (82) including 65 in L and 15 in Markan sections, with 2 added). Apparently Luke found this construction in his sources, his normal usage being εἶπεν πρός. Of doctrinal importance is his use of ὁ κύριος of Jesus in narrative (Matt. (1), Mark (1), Acts (26), Luke (18) including 16 in L, one from Mark, and one added). Its primitive currency is manifest. The same is true of ὁ υἱὸς τοῦ ἀνθρώπου (Acts (1), Matt. (29/30), Mark (14), John (12), Rev. (2), Luke (25/26)). Many scholars will be slow to admit that Luke owes this title exclusively to his sources. But the linguistic facts are significant. Of the examples in Luke seven are taken over from Mark and all the rest (eighteen or nineteen) from Q and L, while in Acts the name occurs once only (vii. 56). The evidence suggests that of himself Luke does not independently use the name, that it was current in the circles from which he derived his sources, perhaps as early as A.D. 40–50, and that the name was no longer used in primitive Christianity when the Third Gospel was compiled. The theological importance of these results, if accepted, is manifest.

Four constructions at the end of the list illustrate the use of a special source. Two consist of vocatives, double and single, of persons and places; and of substantives used as vocatives. The third construction consists of examples of the historical present. Luke omits ninety-two of the 151 examples in Mark. This suggests that he has no partiality for the historical present tense. All the more significant it is that there are twelve examples in contexts which appear to be based on special sources. Finally, as already indicated, Rehkopf lists five examples, all in contexts apparently derived from special sources, of substitutes for the Divine Name in the third person active plural. These are δώσουσιν (vi. 38*b*), ἀπαιτοῦσιν (xii. 20), αἰτήσουσιν (xii. 48*b*), δέξωνται (xvi. 9), and ποιοῦσιν (xxiii. 31*a*). Some of these are open to challenge. They may be impersonal plurals used as the equivalents of a passive. In xvi. 9 J. M. Creed recognises that the subject is really God and that, although the verb is the equivalent for the passive, it is used to avoid naming God. Billerbeck says that God is meant in xvi. 9 and compares vi. 38. If this is so, the passages indicate the use of a source containing Semitisms.[1]

---

[1] In an interesting review of Rehkopf's book (*JTS*, NS XII, 74ff.), A. R. C. Leaney comments on Rehkopf's linguistic arguments, but does not discuss his list of words and phrases illustrative of pre-Lukan speech usage. He doubts whether the Passion narrative is decisive for determining the linguistic character of the Third Gospel, and maintains that the examination of the question of sources is the first step in such an inquiry. He doubts also if the minute examination of two narratives is decisive for the affirmation of a continuous non-Markan narrative.

Among considerations of detail he claims that Lk. iv. 14f. can be understood as a re-writing of Mk. i. 14f. Against this submission is the fact that Lk. iv. 14f. has only five words (out of thirty) parallel to Mk. i. 14f. (none parallel to Mk. i. 15). He maintains that Lk. iv. 22 reflects Mk. vi. 2*b*, although there is no word common to the two passages, and that Lk. iv. 24 'certainly reflects' Mk. vi. 1 (in the use of πατρίς) and is 'clearly parallel' to Mk. vi. 4; but this claim is too slenderly based. In considering Lk. v. 1–11 he points out that already in iv. 38 Peter is a disciple, but does not observe that this verse stands in a passage inserted from Mark, which causes the displacement. He accepts the view that Lk. v. 1–11 is the post-resurrection appearance shared with Jn. xxi. 1–14. He agrees with H. F. D. Sparks (*JTS*, XLIV, 129–38) that Luke's style is strongly influenced by the Septuagint, instancing πορεύεσθαι in Lk. xxii. 22 and αὐτῷ in Lk. xxii. 48*a* (cf. i. 19 and 30). πορεύεσθαι is very frequent in Luke, but whether he took it from the LXX is uncertain; and, as we have seen (p. 25), eighty of the eighty-two examples of εἶπεν αὐτῷ occur in Luke's sources. Other examples of the influence of the LXX Leaney finds in ὁρίζειν in Lk. xxii. 22 and ὁ λεγόμενος in Lk. xxii. 47*a*. πατάσσω (Lk. xxii. 49f.) is also very frequent in the LXX, but, as Rehkopf points out (p. 60), may be a substitute for παίειν (Lk. xxii. 64). Words found in the LXX are to be expected in pre-Lukan speech, but this fact may not

It is obvious from what has been said already that Rehkopf's list must not be used in a mechanical manner. It is a key, but not a master-key, for use in Synoptic research. This indeed is how Rehkopf himself actually uses it. In assessing the evidence his list supplies, we have also to take into account Luke's characteristic usages as indicated by Hawkins, and statistical, stylistic and historical considerations. 'Its value consists in the fact that it enables us to correct some of Hawkins' claims, and that it complies with the searching conditions which Rehkopf lays down...We are in a much better situation to pursue the delicate work of source-criticism than has been possible hitherto.'[1]

EDITORIAL NOTE

Since Dr Taylor wrote the foregoing section and Detached Note, the Proto-Luke hypothesis has met with further criticism, notably from W. G. Kümmel (*Introduction to the New Testament*, pp. 92–5) and E. Earle Ellis (*The Gospel of Luke*, The Century Bible, new ed., pp. 26f.). Kümmel rejects both the Proto-Luke hypothesis and that of a Lukan special source for the Passion narrative. He argues that Luke made Mark the basis of the composition of his Gospel, and followed, on the whole, its sequence. Occasionally, however, he changed the sequence, and when inserting his 'interpolations' into the Markan framework he always omitted a section of Mark, thus interrupting the sequence

be a complete explanation of Luke's style, in particular of xxii. 49, since in this passage there are two Semitisms, εἰ in a direct question and ἐν instrumental. In his discussion of the action of Judas he says, 'In Lk no less than in Mk, therefore, the kiss is a signal', but he does not consider whether a signal is intended by Judas as in Mk. xiv. 44. Mk. xiv. 39–42 (Gethsemane), he suggests, may have been omitted by Luke in order to spare the reputation of the disciples, and Lk. xxii. 35–8 may have been composed by Luke himself. In the latter, however, there is a notable absence of words characteristic of Luke (in Hawkins's list), and Rehkopf includes nine words from the narrative in his own list. Leaney finds remote parallels to Lk. xxii. 53*b* in Lk. iv. 6, 13, and xxi. 24. All these are doubtful claims. Of the book as a whole Leaney says, 'Rehkopf's work has been well and thoroughly done and must be carefully weighed by future workers in this field' (p. 77). This favourable opinion seems strange in the light of Leaney's review as a whole.

[1] Cited from my article, 'Rehkopf's List of Words and Phrases Illustrative of Pre-Lukan Speech Usage', *JTS*, NS xv (1964), 59–62.

of the Markan material. The 'central section' (ix. 51 – xviii. 14) is 'not just a primitive tradition taken over by Luke, but a composition of the Evangelist, who has widened the situation advanced in Mk. x. 1, xi. 1 for the insertion of his disparate material'. Rehkopf, says Kümmel, has failed to demonstrate 'the presence of a connected special tradition in Luke, or even the working together of this special tradition with Q before the insertion of the Markan material'. As for the Passion narrative, Kümmel argues, against Rehkopf, Schürmann and Winter, that 'we must seriously consider the possibility that Luke enriched Mark's passion narrative by orally transmitted features or accounts, or transformed it on the basis of such tradition, so long as no really compelling reasons for the dependence of Luke upon a connected special source in the passion narrative are adduced'. Referring to Dr Taylor's article in *ET*, LXXI, 68ff. on 'Methods of Gospel Criticism', Kümmel claims that 'V. Taylor very recently saw himself forced to admit that Mark presumably furnishes the framework of the Lukan passion narrative'. The article in question, which in substance is reprinted as Part One, section 4, of the present work,[1] does not in fact make such an admission, and the whole of the present work reveals how far Dr Taylor was therefrom.

Like Kümmel, and in line with the prevalent modern tendency, Ellis ascribes to the evangelist himself the major part in the composition of his Gospel.

Luke's own contribution [he writes] must not be underrated...Luke's alteration and omission of parts of Mark show that it, no less than the Q and L traditions, is subservient to Luke's purposes...The primary reason [for the Markan omissions] is that no one document is really the foundation for the third Gospel. All the sources are quarries from which the Evangelist selects and adapts material to serve his own end. The 'Gospel according to Luke' is a considerable achievement, an achievement that in plan, as well as in publication, belongs to Luke.

Ellis regards the task facing the advocates of Proto-Luke as that of establishing by reliable criteria the unity of the source. Of Dr Taylor's attempt to do this in *BTG* he says that 'the unity that he deduces appears to be nothing more than the unity of the Gospel of Luke itself'. Ellis describes Rehkopf's essay as a 'valiant attempt to isolate a pre-Lukan vocabulary that is

[1] See p. 33 n. 2 below.

common to Q and L', but doubts whether 'his methodology is adequate to establish the limits, or the existence, of proto-Luke'.

In their criticisms of Rehkopf both Kümmel and Ellis refer to an article by Schürmann, first published in *Biblische Zeitschrift*, 5 (1961), 266–86, and subsequently reprinted in the author's *Traditionsgeschichtliche Untersuchungen zu den synoptischen Evangelien* (1968), pp. 209–27. It does not appear that Dr Taylor had seen this article, which is an extended review of Rehkopf's *Die lukanische Sonderquelle* and subjects his list of 'Words and Phrases Illustrative of Pre-Lukan Speech Usage' to a most detailed and searching analysis. Commenting on Rehkopf's five criteria,[1] Schürmann points out that to prove negatively that a speech usage is *un*-Lukan does not amount to a positive demonstration that it belongs to a *Proto*-Lukan redaction of Q and L.[2] Un-Lukan words and phrases can only be assigned to a Proto-Lukan redaction when there is a definite and striking agreement as between the Q and L material in their usage. Applying this test, Schürmann reduces Rehkopf's seventy-eight examples to twenty-nine, which he then proceeds to examine individually. He finds that in twenty of these cases the theory of a Proto-Lukan origin is not the most probable explanation of the facts, while in the remaining nine the Proto-Lukan origin is not demonstrable. In view of these 'less encouraging results', Schürmann considers that anyone who wishes to hold on to the theory of a Proto-Lukan redaction must, contrary to the classical Proto-Luke hypothesis, have recourse to the view that it was not a case of a redactor uniformly editing L and Q and firmly combining them, but rather of a compiler loosely joining together the two strata of tradition without giving to his new collection any strong linguistic and stylistic unity. This means that the existence and extent of such a 'Proto-Luke' cannot be determined by means of linguistic and stylistic criteria. Schürmann suggests that the pre-Lukan compiler would, however, betray himself at least in the redactional verses which join the L with the Q sections, and that further progress in the study of Proto-Luke requires a detailed investigation of these redactional connecting verses. Schürmann

[1] See above, p. 24.
[2] The symbol L is used here in the 'British' sense. Rehkopf and Schürmann, of course, use the symbol S. See above, p. 21 n. 1.

does not claim to have refuted the thesis of a pre-Lukan composition of L and Q, but only to have removed for the time being the linguistic–stylistic arguments for the hypothesis, as adduced by Rehkopf.

It is impossible to estimate how far Dr Taylor's confidence in the value of Rehkopf's list would have been shaken had he been able to weigh carefully these arguments of Schürmann. One suspects that he would simply have repeated, even more emphatically, his proviso that 'Rehkopf's list must not be used in a mechanical manner', that it is 'a key, but not a master-key for use in Synoptic research', and that in assessing the evidence it supplies there must also be taken into account various other considerations.[1] So far as the present work is concerned, however, it is worth pointing out that in the above-mentioned article Schürmann does not renounce the views expressed in his three-volume study of Lk. xxii. 7–38 as regards the Lukan Passion narrative. He thinks it likely that in the actual corpus of his Gospel, iv. 31 – xxii. 14, Luke took Mk. i. 21 – xiv. 18a as his chief pattern, but that in the account of the beginning, iii. 1 – iv. 30, and in the Passion narrative, xxii. 15 – xxiv. 9, he adopted a different procedure, since his non-Markan material here offered a parallel narrative to that of Mark, so that Luke was able to combine the two without hesitating to alter or transpose the Markan pattern.[2] Thus Schürmann does not question the existence of a pre-Lukan Passion narrative different from that of Mark, but only the view that such a Passion narrative was a component part of a more extensive 'Proto-Luke'. For Dr Taylor's attitude to this question, see below, p. 125.

4. METHODS OF GOSPEL CRITICISM[3]

In investigating the problem of the Lukan Passion narrative four methods can be used: (1) the numerical or statistical method, (2) the literary or stylistic study, (3) the form-critical approach, and (4) the use of historical criticism. The first two and the fourth

[1] See above, p. 27.
[2] *Traditionsgeschichtliche Untersuchungen zu den synoptischen Evangelien*, p. 210.
[3] This section is a reprint, with some modifications, of Dr Taylor's article, 'Methods of Gospel Criticism', *ET*, LXXI, 68ff. See p. 33 n. 2 below [Ed.].

have a long history behind them and have firmly established themselves in gospel criticism, especially in the distinguishing of sources. The third has to do with the forms in which narratives appear and with the extent to which they have been shaped by communal influences. Its value is disputed, but it raises questions which cannot be ignored.

(1) The *numerical* or *statistical* method is usually employed when comparing parallel narratives in order to determine whether one is or is not the source of the other. The method is especially useful in studying Mark or Q, and has been used by many scholars. J. C. Hawkins's *Horae Synopticae* (2nd ed. 1909) is a mine of information bearing upon these problems. As is well known, Hawkins gives invaluable lists of words and phrases characteristic of each of the Synoptic gospels, points to indications of sources, and makes important statistical observations about the origin and composition of these gospels. Other scholars who have provided factual data include B. S. Easton in *The Gospel according to St Luke* (1926) and P. Parker in *The Gospel before Mark* (1953).

The value of statistical information is beyond doubt. Luke's use of Mark is a case in point. The percentage of Markan words in Lk. iv. 31–44 is 52, in Lk. v. 12 – vi. 11 it is 53.6, and there are similar percentages in Lk. viii. 4 – ix. 50 and Lk. xviii. 15–43, where it rises to 68. In these passages Luke's debt to Mark is generally recognised. Problems arise when the percentage is lower, and here the statistical method has to be supplemented by literary and critical investigations. Lk. vi. 17–19 (many miracles of healing), Lk. xxi. 5–36 (the eschatological discourse), and, above all, the Passion narrative in Lk. xxii. 14 – xxiv. 11, are notable examples. J. M. Creed has reminded us that the numerical method of dealing with words peculiar to each evangelist is not satisfactory without reference to the actual similarities and dissimilarities in each particular case.[1] This requirement applies especially to narratives where the amount of agreement is less than 50 per cent.

The eschatological discourse in Lk. xxi. 5–36 is a test case for

---

[1] *St Luke* (1930), p. 86. This criticism is brought by Creed against my treatment of the Proto-Luke hypothesis in *BTG*. For my reply, see *The Formation of the Gospel Tradition* (2nd ed. 1935), p. 197, where I point out that I have repeatedly observed the principle he mentions.

the validity of the statistical method. F. C. Burkitt argued in *The Beginnings of Christianity*[1] that, while the style of this section is characteristically Lukan, the passage is none the less a version of Mk. xiii. 3–37, and is thus 'a measure of the general faithfulness of "Luke" to his sources'. This weighty opinion is frequently quoted, but it is doubtful if it can be sustained. The first part of the discourse, xxi. 5–11, has a percentage of agreement with Mark amounting to 58.1. This fact, together with stylistic improvements, editorial modifications, and parallel agreements in the order of subject-matter, demonstrates the Markan origin of the passage.[2] The same is true also of the next section, xxi. 12–19, although here it is possible that vv. 16f. are derived from a non-Markan source.[3] But the position is altogether different in xxi. 20–36. Since 1920, four different scholars,[4] writing more or less independently, have maintained that this is a non-Markan section in which Markan passages have been inserted, and they agree that the insertions are to be found in vv. 21*a*, 23*a*, 26*b*–27, and 29–33.[5] The remaining two-thirds of xxi. 20–36 stands out in striking contrast. It includes 178 words, of which 19 only (or 10.6 per cent) are common to Luke and Mark. If admitted, these facts show that Burkitt's argument is delusive, and that therefore it is inadmissible if we use it as a standard by which to judge the composition of the Lukan Passion narrative. They prove that on occasion Luke does insert extracts from Mark into non-Markan sources.

As regards the Passion narrative in Lk. xxii. 14 – xxiv. 53, it is usually said, on the authority of Hawkins, that the percentage of Markan words is 27 as compared with 53 in the earlier parts of Luke.[6] This statement is probably true, but may easily be misleading, for the indubitable Markan words in this long section are not evenly spread over the whole, but are massed together in short passages and narratives. Thus, in xxii. 19*a* twelve words out of fourteen are Markan; in xxii. 22 thirteen out of eighteen; in xxii. 34 eight out of sixteen; in xxii. 46*b* six out of seven; in xxii. 50 ten out of seventeen; in xxii. 52–3*a* twenty-six out of thirty-eight. In the story of the denial (xxii. 54*b*–61) the percentage is almost 50, and in that of the burial (xxiii. 50–4) it is 41.5.

---

[1] *BC*, II, 106ff.
[2] Cf. *BTG*, pp. 102–4.
[3] *Op. cit.* pp. 104–9.
[4] Cf. V. Taylor, *St Mark*, p. 512.
[5] Cf. *BTG*, pp. 110–13.
[6] Cf. *Oxford Studies*, p. 78.

Other Markan passages in xxii. 14 – xxiv. 11 have similar percentages: xxiii. 3 (16/19, i.e. sixteen out of nineteen); xxiii. 26 (11/19); xxiii. 34*b* (6/7); xxiii. 38 (7/11); xxiii. 44f. (17/26); xxiv. 10 (9/21). These are the passages I enumerated in *Behind the Third Gospel*[1] as taken from Mark. It is possible, however, that other passages should be included, for in these there are similar percentages: xxii. 47 (10/14); xxii. 69? (9/16); xxii. 71 (5/15); xxiv. 1–3 (15/32). I do not feel the same confidence about including some of these, but, if they are Markan, it is important to observe that, like xxiii. 26 in the previous list, two of them are the *opening* verses in the narratives to which they belong (xxii. 47; xxiv. 1–3).[2] Further investigation is needed, but if these opening verses are Markan, we should have to conclude that Luke was guided by the Markan order to a degree not yet recognised by protagonists of the Proto-Luke hypothesis. This admission would not destroy the hypothesis, but it would go far to meet the claims of its opponents who contend that Mark supplies the framework of the Lukan Passion narrative.

It will be seen that the percentage of Markan words in the Markan passages in Lk. xxii. 14 – xxiv. 11 is far above the 27 per cent mentioned by Hawkins. In fact, it amounts to considerably over 60 per cent, and is actually in excess of that found in the large Markan sections in the earlier part of Luke. On the other hand, the percentage of such words in the non-Markan parts of the Lukan Passion narrative is very small indeed, amounting to less than 10 per cent. Further, when we allow for words like 'crucify', 'council', and similar words, without which the story could not be told, the percentage is negligible.

It is not claimed that numerical considerations taken by themselves are enough to prove that a special Lukan source is drawn upon in Lk. xxii. 14 – xxiv. 11, but it is suggested that the statistics point definitely in this direction, and that the hypo-

[1] P. 74.
[2] In the article in *ET*, LXXI, 68ff., Dr Taylor included xxii. 39, 66 and xxiii. 33 in his list of 'possibly Markan' passages. Each of these is the opening verse of the narrative to which it belongs, so that the number of such cases amounted to five, not two as above. See p. 119 n. 1 below for Dr Taylor's revised opinion on this point. This modification has the effect of reducing the force of the objection to the Proto-Luke hypothesis which Dr Taylor recognises in the present paragraph [Ed.].

thesis becomes almost a certainty if it is further supported by literary and stylistic criticism. The fact that in some cases, in spite of a high percentage of agreement with Mark, a particular passage appears from linguistic considerations to be non-Markan does not invalidate the numerical argument. It will be argued later that Lk. xxii. 19*a* is a case in point. The position would appear to be that statistical considerations need to be supplemented in some cases by linguistic and literary-critical arguments.

(2) In addition to the statistical method, that of *literary and stylistic criticism* is of much value. H. J. Holtzmann and A. Harnack brought it to a high pitch of usefulness, and it had long been used before their day. Later the method was used by W. Sanday, J. C. Hawkins, B. H. Streeter, and others, in *Oxford Studies in the Synoptic Problem* (1911), and more recently it has been employed with useful results by W. Bussmann in *Synoptische Studien* (1925–31). A notable application of the method can be seen in H. Schürmann's investigation of the Lukan account of the Last Supper in a work of three parts[1] which devotes 436 pages and about 1500 footnotes to the investigation of the thirty-two verses in Lk. xxii. 7–38. Probably no work in any language makes so detailed and so painstaking a use of the literary-critical method. Unlike many who use this method, he combines it with both the numerical and the form-critical methods.

The literary-critical method is concerned with the relationships between two or more writings in respect of grammar, vocabulary, and style. A good example is Harnack's study of Q in Matthew and Luke in *The Sayings of Jesus* (1908) or his investigation of the authorship and sources of Acts in *The Acts of the Apostles* (1909) and *The Date of the Acts and of the Synoptic Gospels* (1911). These works are cited because they remind us of some of the criticisms to which studies of this kind are exposed. While objective in the sense that it deals with facts of language and style, the literary-critical method is open to the charge of subjectivity. A scholar may exaggerate the significance of differences in style, overlook agreements, and misconceive variations of usage and style. In these respects he is exposed to attack

[1] Part I, *Der Paschamahlbericht Lk. xxii. (7–14) 15–18* (1953); Part II, *Der Einsetzungsbericht Lk. xxii. 19–20* (1955); Part III, *Jesu Abschiedsrede Lk. xxii. 21–38* (1957).

by other scholars who read the evidence differently. A good example is J. H. Moulton's essay, 'Some Criticisms on Professor Harnack's "Sayings of Jesus"',[1] in which, as against Harnack, he contends that we cannot assume that Q had simplex verbs, and claims that the papyri must be consulted, that literary tastes differ, that Matthew often abbreviates his sources, and that alternative suggestions are sometimes better. But Moulton does not dispute the validity of the method or deny Harnack's pre-eminence as a scholar. On the contrary, he speaks of him as 'the great master to whom theology owes so much', and as 'the most famous scholar in the greatest University in the world'. Although the literary-critical method has its limitations, it is of considerable value in Synoptic research, especially when it is combined with numerical and form-critical investigations. I have noted this combination in Schürmann's approach, although in his case the use of the literary-critical method predominates. This method is also largely used in Jeremias's *Eucharistic Words of Jesus* and in Rehkopf's *Die lukanische Sonderquelle*. Rejections of the hypothesis of a special Passion narrative in some recent commentaries, with no attempt to use numerical and literary-critical methods, stand out in contrast.

(3) The *form-critical* method calls for no long discussion because, as a constructive method, it is still in its infancy and because the forms which can be distinguished in the Lukan Passion narrative are few. Hitherto form-critics have mainly discussed the transforming influence of the primitive Christian community upon the original tradition and their results have been predominantly negative. Moreover, the limitation of recognised forms to Paradigms or Pronouncement-stories, Novellen or Miracle-stories, and Parables, and the historical problems bound up with Myths and Legends severely restrict the usefulness of the method. Nevertheless, in recent years a constructive use has been made of form-criticism. In 1925 P. Fiebig[2] applied it to the study of Parables and recently J. Jeremias did the same in his *Parables of Jesus*. In 1935 C. H. Dodd discussed the formal characteristics of parables and their

[1] In *The Christian Religion in the Study and the Street* (1919), pp. 71–82.
[2] *Der Erzählungsstil der Evangelien* (1925). We may go back farther, of course, to the discussions of form in A. Jülicher's *Die Gleichnisreden Jesu* (1899–1910).

3-2

setting in life in *The Parables of the Kingdom*. He has also applied the methods of form-criticism to the investigation of the resurrection narratives in a volume of essays in memory of R. H. Lightfoot, edited by D. E. Nineham in *Studies in the Gospels* (1955). The title of the chapter is 'The Appearances of the Risen Christ: An Essay in Form-Criticism of the Gospels', and as an illustration of what can be done it claims attention here.

Dodd reminds us of the distinction made by form-critics between Pronouncement-stories or 'Apophthegms' and the more detailed narratives known as 'Novellen' or 'Tales' and suggests that the two types may be recognised in the stories which follow the account of the discovery of the empty tomb on Easter Day. As examples of 'concise' narratives (Class I) he instances Mt. xxviii. 8–10, 16–20, and Jn. xx. 19–21, and he shows that they follow a common pattern, which may be analysed as follows: A. the situation, B. the appearance, C. the greeting, D. the recognition, and E. the word of command. Examples of the 'circumstantial' narratives (Class II) are the walk to Emmaus (Lk. xxiv. 13–35) and the appearance by the sea (Jn. xxi. 1–14). Besides these there are doubtful or intermediate types, Mk. xvi. 14f., Lk. xxiv. 36–49, Jn. xx. 11–17, and 26–9, but outside the gospels there is little that can be brought into comparison. The 'concise' narratives of Class I bear the marks of a corporate oral tradition. A marked feature of the 'circumstantial' narratives is their association with the eucharistic ideas and practice of the early Church. They include, Dodd thinks, legendary traits, but 'Legend' and 'Myth' are different categories and should not be confused. The narratives which remind us of the Paradigms and Novellen 'merit the same degree of critical consideration, not only in their aspect as witnesses to the faith of the Early Church, but also as ostensible records of things that happened'.[1]

It is obvious that this is an essay of first importance which deserves to be carefully studied. It shows that there is a constructive use of form-criticism which can be of great value in gospel research. It is less useful in investigating the Passion narratives previous to those of the resurrection. For, although there are 'concise' narratives which sometimes end with a saying of Jesus, there are none, except perhaps xxii. 24–7 (true great-

---

[1] *Studies in the Gospels*, p. 35.

ness), which culminate with a pronouncement of Jesus bearing on the life of the primitive community. And the more 'circumstantial' narratives are more elaborate and sometimes as in the story of the crucifixion (xxiii. 33–49) and in that of the arrest (xxii. 47–53) consist of four parts in which the purpose is to describe the course of events. In the account of the trials before Pilate and Herod one story is interwoven into the other which is then resumed (cf. xxiii. 6–12 within xxiii. 1–5 + 13–25). In short, the narrative interest, the desire to tell what happened, is uppermost, along with apologetic and doctrinal motives and an interest in the fulfilment of Scripture. The narratives can only be described broadly as 'stories about Jesus', and form-criticism is of value mainly in bringing out the contrast between them and Paradigms and Novellen. For an estimate of the historical character of these stories we have to rely on the accepted principles of literary and historical criticism.

(4) Like numerical and stylistic methods, *literary and historical criticism* has a long history behind it. It is subjective, but attains increasing objectivity the more its conclusions are widely adopted by competent scholars, although rarely if ever to the exclusion of alternative explanations. In the Passion narrative it is concerned with such questions as the date and occasion of the Last Supper, the nature of the action of Judas, the accounts of the trial scenes, and the details of the burial. The over-riding issue is in what respects the Lukan account, especially when it agrees with that of John, is supplementary or superior to that of Mark, and whether it can be viewed as an independent narrative.

It is beyond question that when two or more of these methods point to the same conclusion great weight is to be attached to it, and when it is supported by three or four of them we reach a result which is almost a moral certainty.

EDITORIAL NOTE

By an interesting coincidence, just as the present work is going to the press, there has appeared as No. 14 in the same series a study by T. Schramm entitled *Der Markus-Stoff bei Lukas: Eine literarkritische und redaktionsgeschichtliche Untersuchung*, which to some extent confirms Dr Taylor's views concerning Luke's method of using his sources. Schramm regards Mark as Luke's main source and is concerned with the manner in which Luke has used it. His conclusion is that where Luke shortens, augments or modifies his Markan source, he is not always trying to include his own theological intentions but is often influenced by variant traditions. Schramm's detailed investigation ends with Lk. xxii. 1–13, which is the point at which Dr Taylor's begins in Part Two below. Whilst not subscribing to the Proto-Luke hypothesis as such, Schramm agrees with Streeter, Taylor, Jeremias, Rehkopf and Schürmann (see above, p. 30) that from xxii. 14 onwards Luke falls back on a (written) special source as the foundation of his narrative, which he enriches with Markan elements.[1]

Two other important works bearing upon aspects of Dr Taylor's study have, unfortunately, appeared too late to be referred to at the relevant points in Part Two. These are *The Trial of Jesus: Cambridge Studies in honour of C. F. D. Moule*, ed. E. Bammel (S.C.M. Press, 1970), and *Verleugnung, Verspottung und Verhör Jesu nach Lukas 22. 54–71*, by G. Schneider (München, 1969). The latter does, with comparable thoroughness and scholarship, for the incidents of the denial, the mocking, and the trial before the priests, what Schürmann and Rehkopf have done for other parts of the Passion narrative, and concludes that in the Passion narrative Luke was working with a written, self-contained, continuous narrative in addition to Mark's. This non-Markan Passion source described, after the arrest, first the bringing of Jesus before the high priest, then the mocking, and then, briefly, the morning hearing before the Sanhedrin with the question of the messiahship. Into this complex it was Luke who first introduced, from Mark, the story of Peter's denial. To this extent, Schneider, though he rejects the Proto-Luke hypothesis as such, is in agreement with Dr Taylor's treatment on pp. 77–84 below.[2]

[1] *Op. cit.* pp. 50f.
[2] For this information about Schneider's book, which I have not myself seen, I am indebted to the comprehensive review by C. F. D. Moule in *JTS*, NS xxii (1971), 194–7 [Ed.].

PART TWO
ANALYSIS AND DETAILED STUDY
OF LUKE XXII–XXIV

Using the methods already described we shall now try to distinguish the Markan and non-Markan elements in the Lukan story of the Passion and resurrection. We shall inquire how far Luke has made use of Mark, and whether he has employed it as his main source. In discussing these questions it will be necessary to view the non-Markan material as a whole; to ask whether it consists of fragments, or whether it is derived from a continuous source, written or oral. Has Luke inserted non-Markan matter into the Markan framework, or has he introduced extracts from Mark into an independent and previously existing Passion narrative? Even if he has had regard to the framework of Mark, is none the less a non-Markan Passion narrative his foundation source?

The investigation resolves itself into an examination of the literary relationship between Lk. xxii–xxiv and Mk. xiv. 1 – xvi. 8.[1] It will be necessary first of all to compare the parallel narratives in the following sections, and then in Part Three to review the Lukan material as a whole. This procedure will compel us to regard some of the conclusions in Part Two as provisional. There will naturally be cases in which a final conclusion is possible only in the light of the whole narrative.

This investigation was undertaken in *BTG*, but in view of objections and further study it is necessary to make it again with a fuller use of statistical, linguistic, and literary-critical methods.

It is generally agreed that Lk. xxii. 1–13 is based on Mark. Nevertheless, it is necessary to study the section again in order to see how Mark has been used, what changes Luke has made, and whether his modifications of Mark are merely editorial or imply the use of an additional source. The section contains three narratives: xxii. 1f.; xxii. 3–6; and xxii. 7–13. Mk. xiv. 3–9 (the anointing at Bethany) is omitted by Luke, probably because of the similar narrative in Lk. vii. 36–50 (the woman in the city).

[1] Mk. xvi. 9–20, the spurious end of the canonical Mark, is of course left out of account. Cf. Taylor, *St Mark*, pp. 610–15.

1. THE PRIESTS' PLOT

(Lk. xxii. 1f.; cf. Mk. xiv. 1f.; Matt. xxvi. 1–5)

[1] Ἤγγιζεν δὲ ἡ ἑορτὴ τῶν ἀζύμων ἡ λεγομένη πάσχα.
[2] καὶ ἐζήτουν οἱ ἀρχιερεῖς καὶ οἱ γραμματεῖς τὸ πῶς ἀνέλωσιν αὐτόν· ἐφοβοῦντο γὰρ τὸν λαόν.

Note The words and phrases common to Luke and Mark, in whole and in part, are underlined. This applies throughout Part Two, sections 1–19.

The percentage of words in common with Mark is high; it amounts to 62.5 per cent. Luke omits a good deal of Mark's account in the interests of abbreviation. Thus he omits the temporal statement 'after two days' in line with his tendency to omit numbers,[1] the reference to the intention to arrest Jesus 'by guile', and the stipulation, 'not during the feast'. The presumption is that he is editing Mark's narrative.

Linguistic features point in the same direction. The account is too brief to supply many examples of Luke's characteristic words, and there is no sign of an earlier source. Luke replaces Mark's ἦν by ἤγγιζεν, a verb he uses frequently.[2] He retains γραμματεῖς, found twenty-two times in Mark, although elsewhere in using the L source he prefers νομικοί and ἄρχοντες, except in xv. 2; xxii. 2, 66; and xxiii. 10. Some of the differences are stylistic. The use of τό followed by the indirect question πῶς ἀνέλωσιν αὐτόν is characteristic,[3] and ἐφοβοῦντο γὰρ τὸν λαόν summarises the end of Mark's narrative.

Summary

It will be seen from the above that xxii. 1f. is wholly dependent on Mark, Luke's modifications being editorial and stylistic.

2. THE TREACHERY OF JUDAS

(Lk. xxii. 3–6; cf. Mk. xiv. 10f.; Matt. xxvi. 14–16)

[3] Εἰσῆλθεν δὲ σατανᾶς εἰς Ἰούδαν τὸν καλούμενον Ἰσκαριώτην, ὄντα ἐκ τοῦ ἀριθμοῦ τῶν δώδεκα, [4] καὶ ἀπελθὼν συνελάλησεν

---

[1] H. J. Cadbury, *The Style and Literary Method of Luke*, pp. 128f.
[2] Luke (18), Acts (6), Matt. (7), Mark (3), Paul (2), rest (5)**.
[3] Schürmann, *Jesu Abschiedsrede*, pp. 11f.

τοῖς ἀρχιερεῦσιν καὶ στρατηγοῖς τὸ πῶς αὐτοῖς παραδῷ αὐτόν. [5] καὶ ἐχάρησαν, καὶ συνέθεντο αὐτῷ ἀργύριον δοῦναι· [6] καὶ ἐξωμολόγησεν καὶ ἐζήτει εὐκαιρίαν τοῦ παραδοῦναι αὐτὸν ἄτερ ὄχλου αὐτοῖς.

The percentage of common words, 45.4, is less than in the preceding narrative, largely because of Luke's additions. Nothing of any moment is omitted from Mark.

Luke explains the treachery of Judas by saying that Satan entered into him. See xxii. 53, where he speaks of 'the power of darkness', and for other references to Satan see also Lk. x. 18; xiii. 16 and xxii. 31, all in L. There is a parallel in Jn. xiii. 2, 'when the devil had already put it into the heart of Judas Iscariot, Simon's son, to betray him'; cf. 1 Cor. ii. 8. The words show that Luke had reflected on the treachery of Judas and the statement may be made in mitigation of his offence. καλούμενος is Lukan. He substitutes ὄντα ἐκ τοῦ ἀριθμοῦ τῶν δώδεκα for Mark's ὁ εἷς τῶν δώδεκα. Luke uses a similar phrase in describing Herod in xxiii. 7, ὄντα καὶ αὐτόν, but he has εἷς τῶν δώδεκα in xxii. 47. His variations from Mark in verse 3 are mainly matters of vocabulary and style and the reference to Satan is doctrinal.

In verse 4 Luke improves the style of the narrative by inserting καί followed by the participle and the finite verb. He is fond of verbs compounded with σύν. Cf. συνελάλησεν, iv. 36, ix. 30, Acts xxv. 12, Matt. xvii. 3, Mk. ix. 4**. στρατηγός (Luke (2), Acts (8)**). τὸ πῶς is used once more (cf. xxii. 2) in verse 4, and a second σύν compound in συνέθεντο (Acts xxiii. 20, Jn. ix. 22**). ἐξομολογέω is used here only with the meaning 'agree'; elsewhere 'acknowledge', 'confess', 'praise'. εὐκαιρία 'opportunity' replaces the adverb (Mark). 'Luke', writes Cadbury,[1] 'shows an aversion to several of the more frequent adverbs and adverbial phrases of Mark.' τοῦ c. infin. is characteristic of Luke and Paul.[2] The normal use is telic, but in Luke and Paul it is often epexegetic ('so as to'). Hawkins[3] speaks of its telic use as 'a decidedly Lucan characteristic'. ἄτερ is found here and in Lk. xxii. 35 only in the

---

[1] *The Style and Literary Method of Luke*, p. 199.
[2] See J. H. Moulton, *A Grammar of New Testament Greek*, I, 216f., II (with W. F. Howard), 448.
[3] *Horae Synopticae* (2nd ed. 1909), p. 48.

New Testament. NEB renders the phrase ἄτερ ὄχλου 'without collecting a crowd'. Apparently it is suggested by ἐν δόλῳ in Mk. xiv. 1, 'with subtlety'.

Summary

All the facts, numerical, linguistic, and stylistic, confirm the view that Mark is Luke's source. He accepts Mark's tradition that Judas betrayed Jesus and accepted a bribe. Whether this was his earlier view depends on how we interpret his account of the arrest in xxii. 47f. In attributing the action of Judas to Satanic influence he appears to reflect Johannine tradition (Jn. xiii. 2), and this allusion may be his attempt to reconcile two different views.

3. PREPARATIONS FOR THE PASSOVER

(Lk. xxii. 7–13; cf. Mk. xiv. 12–16; Matt. xxvi. 17–19)

[7] Ἦλθεν δὲ ἡ ἡμέρα τῶν ἀζύμων, ἐν ᾗ ἔδει θύεσθαι τὸ πάσχα, [8] καὶ ἀπέστειλεν Πέτρον καὶ Ἰωάννην εἰπών· πορευθέντες ἑτοιμάσατε ἡμῖν τὸ πάσχα, ἵνα φάγωμεν. [9] οἱ δὲ εἶπαν αὐτῷ· ποῦ θέλεις ἑτοιμάσωμεν; [10] ὁ δὲ εἶπεν αὐτοῖς· ἰδοὺ εἰσελθόντων ὑμῶν εἰς τὴν πόλιν συναντήσει ὑμῖν ἄνθρωπος κεράμιον ὕδατος βαστάζων· ἀκολουθήσατε αὐτῷ εἰς τὴν οἰκίαν εἰς ἣν εἰσπορεύεται, [11] καὶ ἐρεῖτε τῷ οἰκοδεσπότῃ τῆς οἰκίας· λέγει σοι ὁ διδάσκαλος· ποῦ ἐστιν τὸ κατάλυμα ὅπου τὸ πάσχα μετὰ τῶν μαθητῶν μου φάγω; [12] κἀκεῖνος ὑμῖν δείξει ἀνάγαιον μέγα ἐστρωμένον· ἐκεῖ ἑτοιμάσατε. [13] ἀπελθόντες δὲ εὗρον καθὼς εἰρήκει αὐτοῖς, καὶ ἡτοίμασαν τὸ πάσχα.

The percentage of words in common with Mark, 65.2, is very high indeed, and, as in the two preceding narratives, Luke's modifications are matters of vocabulary and style. From this point onwards we have the advantage of H. Schürmann's meticulous linguistic examination of Lk. xxii. 7–38.[1]

In the opening verse, as often, Luke replaces Mark's καί with δέ. Schürmann points out that out of almost 400 cases of καί in

---

[1] See above, p. 18 n. 2.

Mark, Luke has improved approximately 100.[1] ἦλθεν is placed first and, as frequently, Luke reduces Mark's double temporal statement by replacing πρώτῃ and ὅτε τὸ πάσχα ἔθυον by the nominative and the relative pronoun. Instead of Mark's impersonal plural ἔθυον he has ἐν ᾗ ἔδει θύεσθαι τὸ πάσχα in accordance with his habit of stressing the need to observe prescribed rules and customs.[2] The effect of these editorial changes is to improve the opening sentence.

In Luke the initiative is taken by Jesus. He replaces Mark's historic present by ἀπέστειλεν, and either from oral tradition or his usage in Acts[3] names the two disciples 'Peter and John', adding the participle εἰπών and a second participle πορευθέντες with imperatival force ('Go'). The question of the two disciples is given in the abbreviated form, 'Where do you want us to make ready?'

In introducing the instructions given to Peter and John, Luke again replaces the historic present (λέγει) by εἶπεν and inserts ἰδού, a word which Matthew and he use frequently. He omits Mark's ὑπάγετε, a verb found only five times in Luke and never in Acts, and improves the style by using the genitive absolute εἰσελθόντων ὑμῶν. συναντήσει[4] is another σύν compound. His substitution of εἰς τὴν οἰκίαν εἰς ἣν εἰσπορεύεται is a simplification and improvement of Mark's ὅπου ἐὰν εἰσέλθῃ. The only passage in which Luke has ὅπου ἐάν with the subjunctive is ix. 57 (Q).

In verse 11 Luke and Mark are in very close agreement. The aorist imperative εἴπατε, which Luke rarely uses,[5] is replaced by ἐρεῖτε (frequent in Luke), a future which here has imperatival force. τῆς οἰκίας is added to τῷ οἰκοδεσπότῃ, ὅτι and μου are omitted and σοι is inserted. In verses 12f. the variations are small and clearly editorial. κἀκεῖνος is more precise and ἕτοιμον (Mark) is omitted as unnecessary. καί paratactic is replaced by δέ, and as elsewhere[6] Luke prefers a verb compounded with ἀπό to one with

---

[1] *Der Paschamahlbericht*, p. 76; cf. Hawkins, *Horae Synopticae*, pp. 150–2; Cadbury, *The Style and Literary Method of Luke*, pp. 142–7.
[2] Lk. i. 15; ii. 21ff.; xi. 42; xiii. 14; Acts iii. 1; v. 12; xxi. 20; etc.
[3] Acts iii. 1, 3, 11; iv. 13, 19; viii. 14.
[4] Luke (3), Acts (2), Heb. (2)**.
[5] Lk. x. 10 (Q); xiii. 32 (L); Acts xxiv. 20.
[6] Cf. Cadbury, *The Style and Literary Method of Luke*, p. 202.

ἐξ. He also reduces the finite verbs in his source by using ἀπελθόν-τες. With εἰρήκει compare his use of the pluperfect elsewhere in Luke and Acts.[1]

Summary

It is clear that equally with xxii. 1f. and 3–6, Lk. xxii. 7–13 is derived from Mark with no more than editorial and stylistic changes. Schürmann[2] describes this conclusion as 'a moral certainty'.

As observed at the outset, it might seem unnecessary to examine the three narratives in xxii. 1–13 in detail when this view of its origin is so widely accepted. But, as we have seen, the examination of the section is a necessary discipline if we want to see how Luke uses Mark. It is a salutary warning against the danger of too readily describing sections which are substantially non-Markan as 'editorial revisions of Mark'. Lk. xxii. 1–13, along with iv. 31–44; v. 12 – vi. 11; viii. 4 – ix. 50; xviii. 15–43 and xx. 1 – xxi. 19, shows that when Luke draws upon Mark, he follows his source with considerable fidelity despite stylistic and other changes. It is obviously necessary to explain why, with certain exceptions, his procedure in xxii. 14 – xxiv is so different.

Note

It is important to observe that in the three preceding Markan narratives words characteristic of Luke (Hawkins) and those present in Rehkopf's list are not significant in source criticism unless they are supported by additional arguments. The former are merely editorial; the latter are not sufficient to imply the use of a non-Markan source. Easton,[3] however, observes that Luke corresponds closely with Mark in vv. 2 and 5, but not otherwise. The non-Markan material, he says, is complete in itself and is from L. It is doubtful if we can go so far: ἀναιρέω, λαός, καλού-μενος, τό followed by an indirect question, two verbs compounded with σύν, and τοῦ c. infin. can all be explained as Lukan embel-lishments of Mark. The few words from Rehkopf's list (σατανᾶς, εἶπεν c. dat., and ἐρεῖτε), especially σατανᾶς, may indicate

---

[1] Cf. xi. 22 and xix. 15 (Q); iv. 29; viii. 2; and xvi. 20 (L); also viii. 29, 38; xxiii. 35 and 49, of which the last two may be from L. See, also, Acts viii. 24; xiii. 34; xvii. 28; and xx. 38.

[2] *Der Paschamahlbericht*, p. 104.

[3] *St Luke*, pp. 316f.

knowledge of other sources, but hardly more.[1] These comments on Luke's use of Mark in xxii. 1–13 reveal points to be considered when his use of non-Markan sources is in question.

4. THE LAST SUPPER

(Lk. xxii. 14–20; cf. Mk. xiv. 22–5;
Matt. xxvi. 26–9; 1 Cor. xi. 23–5)

[14] Καὶ ὅτε ἐγένετο ἡ ὥρα, ἀνέπεσεν, καὶ οἱ ἀπόστολοι σὺν αὐτῷ. [15] καὶ εἶπεν πρὸς αὐτούς· ἐπιθυμίᾳ ἐπεθύμησα τοῦτο τὸ πάσχα φαγεῖν μεθ᾽ ὑμῶν πρὸ τοῦ με παθεῖν· [16] λέγω γὰρ ὑμῖν ὅτι οὐκέτι οὐ μὴ φάγω αὐτὸ ἕως ὅτου πληρωθῇ ἐν τῇ βασιλείᾳ τοῦ θεοῦ. [17] καὶ δεξάμενος ποτήριον εὐχαριστήσας εἶπεν· λάβετε τοῦτο καὶ διαμερίσατε εἰς ἑαυτούς. [18] λέγω γὰρ ὑμῖν ὅτι οὐ μὴ πίω ἀπὸ τοῦ νῦν ἀπὸ τοῦ γενήματος τῆς ἀμπέλου ἕως οὗ ἡ βασιλεία τοῦ θεοῦ ἔλθῃ.

[19a] Καὶ λαβὼν ἄρτον εὐχαριστήσας ἔκλασεν καὶ ἔδωκεν αὐτοῖς λέγων Τοῦτό ἐστιν τὸ σῶμά μου [[19b] τὸ ὑπὲρ ὑμῶν διδόμενον· τοῦτο ποιεῖτε εἰς τὴν ἐμὴν ἀνάμνησιν. [20] καὶ τὸ ποτήριον ὡσαύτως μετὰ τὸ δειπνῆσαι, λέγων Τοῦτο τὸ ποτήριον ἡ καινὴ διαθήκη ἐν τῷ αἵματί μου, τὸ ὑπὲρ ὑμῶν ἐκχυννόμενον.]

The Lukan narrative consists of two parts, xxii. 14–18 which is marked by a strong eschatological interest, and xxii. 19–20 which describes the institution of the Eucharist. Since verses 19b–20 are omitted by the Western text of D and its allies, and are widely regarded as an interpolation based on 1 Cor. xi. 23–5, it will be well to examine verses 14–18 and 19–20 separately. If the interpolation hypothesis is sound, 19a must belong to 14–18 and 14–19a must then be regarded as a whole constituting Luke's account of the Supper; but since the subject-matter of 19a so obviously agrees with that of 19b–20, it will prove advantageous to treat 19–20 as a separate unit. The section 14–18 will be considered first.

[1] Cf. T. Schramm, *Der Markus-Stoff bei Lukas* (see above, pp. 37 f.), pp. 182–4. Schramm concludes that Lk. xxii. 1–13 is based solely on Mark, apart from the reference to Satan in verse 3, which he describes as 'ein Motiv seiner Sondertradition' [Ed.].

(a) Lk. xxii. 14–18

This section differs considerably from the three narratives in xxii. 1–13 in respect of its Markan element. Even if we add 19a to it, only thirty-four words out of ninety-one (37.3 per cent) are common to Luke and Mark, and without this half-verse the Markan words are twenty-two out of seventy-seven (28.5 per cent). These percentages are low, since quite independent accounts of the Supper might be expected to have a number of words in common, and also because elsewhere Luke follows his sources closely when, as in the present case, they contain sayings of Jesus.[1] On statistical grounds we are entitled to suspect that xxii. 14–18 is based on a non-Markan source.

Linguistic considerations support this view. On these grounds Schürmann concludes that 15–18 is non-Markan, but suggests that 14 is an edited version of Mk. xiv. 17–18a. Obviously these views call for examination, and this will now be undertaken.

Verse 14

Verse 14 may be considered first. Schürmann holds that this verse is Markan.[2] He submits that of himself Luke prefers ὅτε δὲ ἐγένετο to καὶ ὅτε ἐγένετο and maintains that ἀνέπεσεν is a correction of the impersonal plural ἀνακειμένων followed by εἶπεν, by which Jesus is first included with the disciples and then distinguished from them. He also suggests that Luke has replaced μετά with his favourite σύν, and that ἀπόστολος belongs to his Pauline vocabulary. These suggestions hardly amount to a proof that in 14 Luke's source is Mark.[3] They point to the use of a source, but this source may be non-Markan. Rehkopf takes this view and claims that ἀναπίπτω and ἀπόστολος belong to pre-Lukan usage.[4] In part the vocabulary is due to Luke himself, since 14 contains words characteristic of his style. Hawkins's lists include ἀπόστολος, σύν, ἀπὸ τοῦ νῦν, and γίνομαι used with ἡμέρα (cf. xxii. 6).[5]

Was 14 preceded by a statement or narrative to which ἡ ὥρα

[1] Cf. Cadbury, *The Style and Literary Method of Luke*, p. 124.
[2] *Der Paschamahlbericht*, pp. 104–10.
[3] So also P. Winter, *NTS*, II (1956), 208; J. Jeremias, *The Eucharistic Words of Jesus*, p. 99 n. 1.
[4] See his list, *LS*, pp. 91–106.
[5] *Horae Synopticae*, pp. 15–29.

48

referred? Schürmann suggests that a lost original introduction to 15–18 has been replaced by the evangelist by Mk. xiv. 12–18*a* (preparations for the Passover) = Lk. xxii. 7–14. Believing that verse 14 is non-Markan, I would prefer to say that the original introduction, which Schürmann calls X, has been replaced by Mk. xiv. 12–16. But whether we find a gap before Lk. xxii. 14 or 15 we have still to explain why the introduction has been replaced. Elsewhere[1] I have tentatively suggested that, influenced by Mk. xiv. 12, Luke abandoned the implication of his source, contained in the words, 'I have greatly desired to eat this Passover' (Lk. xxii. 15), that the Supper preceded the Passover, as in Jn. xviii. 28 and xix. 14, and adopted the Markan view that the Supper was the actual meal. This suggestion is speculative, but it has the merit of a possible and even probable explanation of 'the gap' and in no way rules out the view that Passover associations were in the mind of Jesus at the Supper.

Verses 15–18

Verses 15–18 may be taken together because of signs that they form a unit of tradition. Verse 18, for example, is not loosely appended to the rest, like the parallel version of the saying in Mk. xiv. 25. Schürmann has examined in great detail the linguistic and formal characteristics of the section, and has maintained that Luke has lightly edited a non-Markan source independent of Mark.[2] Among the signs of his activity he points to εἶπεν πρός *c. acc.* which, he suggests, has perhaps replaced an original εἶπεν αὐτοῖς, the phrase ἐπιθυμίᾳ ἐπεθύμησα, imitated from the Septuagint, the compound verb διαμερίσατε used presumably instead of the simplex verb, the articular infinitive πρὸ τοῦ με παθεῖν, πληρωθῇ, ἀπὸ τοῦ νῦν which may be a substitute for οὐκέτι, ἀπό instead of ἐκ before τοῦ γενήματος τῆς ἀμπέλου, and ἕως οὗ (or ὅτου) with the subjunctive.

Schürmann's argument from the form of 15–18 is impressive. He points out that there is a parallelism between 15f. and 17f. marked by the presence of λέγω γὰρ ὑμῖν and ἕως ὅτου (οὗ) in 16 and 18, a construction not frequent in Luke, which suggests the use of a Semitic source.[3] This argument bears on the origin

---

[1] *BTG*, pp. 37–40, 177–80.   [2] *Der Paschamahlbericht*, pp. 1–74.
[3] Cf. Cadbury, *The Style and Literary Method of Luke*, p. 88; Jeremias, *The Eucharistic Words of Jesus*, pp. 160–4.

of the saying in 18, which otherwise contains a considerable number of words (fourteen out of twenty-one) common to Luke and Mark. It may be non-Markan. Several of the phrases, 'the fruit of the vine' and 'the kingdom of God', might be expected in independent versions of the saying, and there is a difference at the end, where Luke has 'until the kingdom of God shall come' instead of Mark's 'until the day when I drink it new in the kingdom of God'. This double reference to the kingdom is another example of the parallelism between 15f. and 17f. Jeremias comes to the same conclusion,[1] pointing out Semitisms in 15–18 and apparent improvements in the Greek made by Luke in a pre-Lukan source.

Summary

In view of statistical, linguistic, and structural characteristics in Lk. xxii. 14–18, there is good reason to trace the passage to a non-Markan source. This conclusion is supported by the eschatological interest of the passage, in which it differs from other accounts of the Supper apart from 1 Cor. xi. 26 ('until he come'). Whether Luke included 19a in this complex depends on the view taken of 19b–20. To this passage we now turn, provisionally examining 19–20 as a whole.

(b) Lk. xxii. 19–20

The text of 19b–20

Lk. xxii. 19b–20 is read by P75, all Greek uncial MSS except D all the Versions except a few MSS of the Old Latin and sy^s and sy^c, Marcion, Justin, and probably Tatian. It is omitted by D a d ff^2 i l, also by b and e, sy^s and sy^c; see my *Text of the New Testament*, pp. 91–3. Schürmann has fully examined the textual evidence in *Biblica*, xxxii (1951). In *Der Einsetzungsbericht* (1955) he discusses in the greatest detail the linguistic and stylistic phenomena and comes to the conclusion that Paul derived 1 Cor. xi. 23–5 from an earlier liturgical source. If it can be established, this hypothesis is of the utmost importance, since it would leave open the possibility that Lk. xxii. 19–20 was also drawn from this

---

[1] *Op. cit.* pp. 160–4. With reference to the account of the Eucharist, C. H. Dodd says that Luke's dependence on Mark as a source at this point is 'more than doubtful', *HTFG*, p. 50.

source, and not, as many scholars believe, from 1 Cor. Jeremias also comes to the same conclusion. He examines eighteen other passages in Luke which are omitted by D and its allies and maintains that, with two possible but not certain exceptions (Lk. xxiv. 36 and 40), they are genuine elements in Luke. This conclusion strengthens the case for the genuineness of 19*b*–20. Since Westcott and Hort's discussion of 1881 most British scholars explain the passage as an interpolation from 1 Cor. xi. 23–5, but F. G. Kenyon, S. C. E. Legg, and C. S. C. Williams, with many continental scholars, accept it as genuine. The trend is in this direction.[1]

The linguistic features of Lk. xxii. 19–20 are discussed below, but first it is necessary to examine the Markan element in these verses and the origin of 1 Cor. xi. 23–5.

The distribution of Markan words, underlined on p. 47, is remarkable. In 19*a* they amount to twelve out of fourteen; in 19*b*–20*a* to eight out of twenty-eight; and in 20*b* to three out of four. Each of these parts must be considered separately.

Lk. xxii. 19a

In *BTG* I described the Markan origin of this passage as unquestionable.[2] And so it is, if we pay regard to its numerical aspects only. Schürmann thinks it is non-Markan. He suggests that ἐσθιόντων αὐτῶν (Mk. xiv. 22) may have been omitted as unsuitable to the Lukan context, and that εὐχαριστήσας is un-

---

[1] A. Vööbus, approaching the problem from the direction of what he calls 'motif-history and cult-tradition', has recently defended the originality of the 'shorter text'. Assuming that Lk. xxii. 24–7 is taken over from Mk. x. 41–5 and transplanted by Luke into the context of the Supper, Vööbus argues that 'it is preposterous to believe that the author of the longer text, reproducing a tradition preferred by him, indulged in an interpretative treatment in which he deliberately opted to omit the essential portion – the saying on the λύτρον...It is certain that the longer text could not have been Luke's version of the words of institution' ('A New Approach to the Problem of the Shorter and Longer Text in Luke', *NTS*, xv (1969), 457ff.). Dr Taylor, of course, would not have accepted the premiss of this argument, the dependence of Luke on Mark at this point (see below, pp. 61–4). If Lk. xxii. 19–20 is inconsistent with xxii. 27, as Vööbus claims, the separate origin of vv. 19–20, as compared with vv. 14–18 (see below, pp. 57–8), would help to explain such inconsistency [Ed.].

[2] *BTG*, p. 37.

Lukan, since usually Luke uses it with the dative. Here it is used absolutely and has the technical sense of speaking the eucharistic prayer of thanksgiving. He doubts if Luke would have omitted εὐλογήσας and λάβετε if he had found them in his source. λέγων, he suggests, is perhaps an assimilation to verse 20 in the interests of symmetry.[1] These arguments seem slender when twelve words out of fourteen are common to Luke and Mark. There are, however, stronger things to be said. (a) It is strange that an interpolator, if he began to operate at 19b, should so conveniently find an adjectival participle (τὸ ὑπὲρ ὑμῶν διδόμενον) to describe τὸ σῶμά μου. (b) The vocabulary of 19a, in its references to taking, breaking, and distributing bread, contains words (λαβὼν ἄρτον, ἔκλασεν, and ἔδωκεν) which would naturally appear in any account of the institution of the Eucharist. (c) 19a has nine words in common with 1 Cor. xi. 23b–24a, ὁ Κύριος Ἰησοῦς ἐν τῇ νυκτὶ ᾗ παρεδίδετο ἔλαβεν ἄρτον καὶ εὐχαριστήσας ἔκλασεν καὶ εἶπεν· τοῦτό μού ἐστιν τὸ σῶμα.[2] (d) G. D. Kilpatrick's suggestion,[3] that 19a was added as a cue 'which the faithful would know how to supplement, but which would tell the uninitiated little', is exposed to the objection that the secret is given away in 'This is my Body'.

For these reasons Schürmann is justified in concluding that 19a comes from a non-Markan source, provided he can show that in 19b–20 Luke is drawing upon such a source. We turn then to examine 19b–20 in order to see if this supposition is justified.

Lk. xxii. 19b–20

The text in 1 Cor. xi. 24b–25 parallel to Lk. xxii. 19b–20 is as follows: τὸ ὑπὲρ ὑμῶν· τοῦτο ποιεῖτε εἰς τὴν ἐμὴν ἀνάμνησιν. [25] ὡσαύτως καὶ τὸ ποτήριον μετὰ τὸ δειπνῆσαι, λέγων· τοῦτο τὸ ποτήριον ἡ καινὴ διαθήκη ἐστὶν ἐν τῷ ἐμῷ αἵματι· τοῦτο ποιεῖτε, ὁσάκις ἐὰν πίνητε, εἰς τὴν ἐμὴν ἀνάμνησιν.[2]

It will be seen that the words common to Luke and 1 Cor. are numerous. They amount to twenty-six out of thirty-seven (70.2 per cent) and, if we take account of the whole of 1 Cor. xi. 23–5, to thirty-five out of sixty-eight (51.4 per cent). It is not at all surprising that the opinion that Lk. xxii. 19b–20 is an interpola-

---

[1] Cf. *Der Einsetzungsbericht*, pp. 43–9.
[2] The words found also in Luke are underlined.
[3] *JTS*, XLVII (1946), 49–56.

tion from 1 Cor. is so widely held. But are Luke and Paul dependent on an earlier liturgical source used by them in common? It will clear the ground if we consider this hypothesis.

Schürmann endorses the view held by many scholars that the references to 'receiving' and 'handing on' in 1 Cor. xi. 23a are rabbinical terms which describe the transmission of a tradition. Paul traces the tradition to Jesus himself. He is not speaking of a revelation made by him, as in Gal. i. 12. Schürmann supports this view by pointing out that the form of 1 Cor. xi. 23–5 resembles the narratives of the Synoptic gospels. An immediate revelation, he maintains, would not have been described in this manner, and he adds further that nowhere else in Luke are the Pauline epistles quoted.

This argument goes a long way in suggesting that Paul is quoting from a pre-Pauline source, and Schürmann supports it by pointing to significant linguistic features in 1 Cor. xi. 23b–25.[1] Among these are: (a) εὐχαριστήσας, which, like Luke, Paul normally uses with the dative, but here uses absolutely; (b) καὶ εἶπεν, which does not introduce a quotation in his epistles; (c) τὸ ὑπὲρ ὑμῶν, the article with a prepositional phrase, is a common Pauline construction[2] which cannot be translated back into Aramaic[3] and here may be a recast of the source, in which Luke's τὸ ὑπὲρ ὑμῶν διδόμενον is probably more original. Again (d) τὸ σῶμα τοῦ Χριστοῦ is used by Paul of the Christian community, except in the eucharistic context of 1 Cor. x. 16. (e) ἀνάμνησις is found in Paul here only. Schürmann admits that this is not to say much, since the word occurs elsewhere in the New Testament only in Heb. x. 3, but suggests that we should expect him to have written μνείαν ποιεῖν (cf. Rom. i. 9, etc.). (f) ὡσαύτως καί is probably more original than καί...ὡσαύτως (Luke). In xx. 31 Luke has ὡσαύτως δὲ καί and καί...ὡσαύτως may be the result of pre-Lukan redaction. (g) μετὰ τό with the infinitive is found in Paul here only, but he has μετά with the accusative in Gal. i. 18 and iii. 17 (cf. Tit. iii. 10). (h) Paul has δειπνεῖν nowhere else. (i) The New Covenant (Jer. xxxi. 31) is not elsewhere connected with the death of Christ, and (j) 'blood' (with a sacrificial

---

[1] *Der Einsetzungsbericht*, pp. 9–14, 17–30.
[2] Cf. 1 Cor. ii. 11; xi. 24; xv. 10; 2 Cor. i. 18; v. 2; vii. 12; viii. 22; ix. 3; Gal. ii. 3; 1 Thess. ii. 1; Col. iv. 12; Philem. 6.
[3] Cf. G. Dalman, *Jesus-Jeshua*, p. 132.

meaning) is connected with the New Covenant of Jer. xxxi. 31, which is not constituted by a sacrifice. (*k*) τοῦτο τὸ ποτήριον: Paul has οὗτος etc. *after* the noun forty-nine times, before five times (according to Gersdorf).

Schürmann recognises that in themselves these unusual elements in the usage of Paul are not all decisive,[1] but submits that the presence of so many in the narrow space of three verses points to pre-Pauline tradition. He also comments on a slight difference between Lk. xxii. 19*b* and 1 Cor. xi. 24*b* in the words of Jesus τοῦτο ποιεῖτε εἰς τὴν ἐμὴν ἀνάμνησιν. In Luke, he submits, the words are first and foremost a command to repeat the rite, although its memorial aspect is also implied, but in 1 Cor. they have more strongly the character of a command to remember the Lord whose death the Corinthians proclaim in the acts of eating and drinking 'until he comes'. This argument is not linguistic but is an interpretation of the Lukan and Pauline narratives.

It must be allowed, I think, that Schürmann makes out a good case for the hypothesis that in 1 Cor. xi. 23–5 Paul is editing an earlier liturgical source. Jeremias comes to the same conclusion quoting much the same linguistic phenomena.[2] 'The account of the Lord's Supper', he writes, 'has idioms foreign to Paul.' This conclusion is of first importance; it means that Luke is not necessarily reproducing 1 Cor. xi. 24*b*–25, but may be drawing upon this pre-Pauline liturgical source. The case for this claim must now be examined.

Both Schürmann and Jeremias conclude that Luke is dependent on the pre-Pauline liturgical source.

Schürmann[3] discusses five differences between Luke and Paul and maintains that in four out of five cases Luke gives the original text of the source. Thus, he prefers Luke's τὸ ὑπὲρ ὑμῶν διδόμενον to Paul's characteristic construction τὸ ὑπὲρ ὑμῶν,[4] and Luke's emphasis on repeating the rite in 19*b*, his omission of the copula in 20*a*,[5] and his ἐν τῷ αἵματί μου instead of Paul's ἐν τῷ ἐμῷ

---

[1] Little is gained, for example, by pointing to words (e.g. ἀνάμνησις and δειπνεῖν) found in Paul only in 1 Cor. xi. 24*b*–25.

[2] *The Eucharistic Words of Jesus*, p. 104.

[3] *Der Einsetzungsbericht*, pp. 17–42.

[4] See p. 53 n. 2. τὸ ὑπὲρ ὑμῶν διδόμενον has sacrificial associations.

[5] Luke generally inserts the copula when it is wanting in Mark or Matt. Cf. Cadbury, *The Style and Literary Method of Luke*, p. 149.

αἵματι.[1] In a fifth case Paul's ὡσαύτως καί is preferred to Luke's καί... ὡσαύτως in view of similar phrases in his Gospel.[2] In all five cases Lukan editing of 1 Cor. xi. 24*b*–25 is the less probable alternative. These conclusions are reached by comparing the words and phrases of Luke and Paul with the normal usages of these writers.

Jeremias[3] lists *un-Lukan* features in 19*b*–20 and claims that these show that the passage was not composed by Luke himself.[4] In addition to the absence of the copula mentioned by Schürmann,[5] he cites as un-Lukan: ὑπέρ, which occurs twice in 19*b*–20 and once more in ix. 50*, but is frequently found in the Pauline epistles in connexion with the atoning work of Christ; ἀνάμνησις, here only in Luke, whereas μνημόσυνον is used in Acts x. 4; the article before ποτήριον in 20 when in 17 and 19*a* ποτήριον and ἄρτος are anarthrous; ἐμός used attributively in 19 as nowhere else in Luke; and τὸ... ἐκχυννόμενον in the nominative in 20*b* although it qualifies αἵματι. These features, especially the last named, are usually held to support the view that Lk. xxii. 19*b*–20 is an interpolation from 1 Cor. xi. 23–5, but, as Jeremias points out,[6] the situation is very different if 19*b*–20 is a liturgical formula. In a liturgical source, he suggests, the nominative (instead of the dative) might well be found, and the want of textual variants shows that nobody was offended by it in the early Church. He maintains that the un-Lukan style of the passage is no valid argument against its originality, and, using a phrase of Dibelius,[7] describes it as a 'third variant' on the liturgical formula relating to the Eucharist.[8] In support of this argument it may be noted that, in contrast to xxii. 14–18, there are no characteristic Lukan words in xxii. 19–20.

[1] Paul has ἐμός 22 times, Luke 3 (ix. 26; xv. 31; xxii. 19).
[2] E.g. ὁμοίως (δὲ) καί, v. 10; x. 32; xxii. 36; ὡσαύτως δὲ καί, xx. 31; καθὼς καί, xi. 1; οὕτως καί, xi. 30; xvii. 26. Schürmann, *Der Einsetzungsbericht*, p. 35, suggests that redaction has taken place in the pre-Lukan source itself and is pre-Lukan.
[3] *The Eucharistic Words of Jesus*, pp. 154f.
[4] G. D. Kilpatrick, *JTS*, XLVII (1946), 51, argues that the un-Lukan features favour the view that Lk. xxii. 19*b*–20 is an interpolation from 1 Cor. xi. 23–5.
[5] See p. 54 above.
[6] *The Eucharistic Words of Jesus*, p. 155.
[7] *From Tradition to Gospel*, p. 210.   [8] Jeremias, *op. cit.* p. 156.

What is to be said concerning this hypothesis? Undoubtedly Schürmann and Jeremias present a strong case, since it is suggested by linguistic phenomena in both I Cor. xi. 23–5 and Lk. xxii. 19b–20. Many British scholars find it difficult to abandon Westcott and Hort's explanation of Lk. xxii. 19b–20, and in view of the large common element in Luke and I Cor. will hesitate to accept the hypothesis of a 'third variant'. At first sight διδόμενον does look like a Lukan addition to Paul's τὸ ὑπὲρ ὑμῶν and the use of ὡσαύτως and μετὰ τὸ δειπνῆσαι by both writers seems to suggest dependence. But, as we have seen, the differences are striking, especially when the same words and phrases are to be expected even in independent narratives of the Supper. Moreover, a generation of research has shaken our confidence in Hort's explanation of Western omissions in Lk. xxii–xxiv and similar earlier passages in Luke. Further, it is difficult to accept his suggestion[1] that an interpolator wished to remove the apparent order, Cup, Bread, in the shorter text, since he could more easily have secured this purpose by the omission of verse 17. Jeremias prefers to think that Lk. xxii. 19b–20 was omitted in order to preserve the *arcanum* of the eucharistic rite.[2] This suggestion is hypothetical, but it is strongly supported and widely illustrated in early Christian and non-Christian literature,[3] and in the New Testament itself. The problem is one of balancing conflicting arguments, no new difficulty in New Testament research. On balance, it is probable that Schürmann and Jeremias are justified in claiming the originality of Lk. xxii. 19b–20 and its source in earlier ecclesiastical usage, presumably at Antioch in the decade A.D. 30–40. This source was probably current in written form and was used independently by Paul and Luke and to some extent adapted by them.

Lk. xxii. 20b, τὸ ὑπὲρ ὑμῶν ἐκχυννόμενον

This phrase, as the underlining shows, has three of its four words in common with Mk. xiv. 24 but differs from Mark in reading ὑμῶν instead of πολλῶν. It is absent from I Cor. xi. The passage

---

[1] *The New Testament in the Original Greek, Notes*, pp. 63f.
[2] *The Eucharistic Words of Jesus*, p. 158.
[3] Jeremias has greatly extended the evidence in a new chapter entitled 'The Influence of Worship upon the Transmission of the Eucharistic Texts', in the latest edition of his book. See pp. 106–37 in the English version.

is too brief for numerical and linguistic arguments to be significant, although it is to be noted that it places the prepositional
phrase before the participle. Its source is either Mark or the
pre-Lukan account embodied in Luke. Schürmann argues at
length for its Markan origin,[1] but it is difficult to believe that
Luke would have reproduced it in the *nominative*, when it clearly
qualifies the dative αἵματι. So far as it goes, this is an argument for
ascribing it to the pre-Lukan source where, according to
Jeremias,[2] the want of concord would not be felt to be offensive,
while Luke might carry it over in fidelity to his source. This is
probably what happened, but this suggestion can be no more than
a scientific guess.

Summary (Lk. xxii. 14–20)

From the foregoing discussion the conclusion suggested is that
Lk. xxii. 14–20 is a combination of two sources, the L source in
verses 14–18 and a pre-Lukan liturgical source in verses 19–20.
Verse 19a may be a Markan addition, but it might be drawn, as
Schürmann contends, from the pre-Lukan source. It is certainly
strange that, after inserting a passage from Mark, Luke should
switch over to a different source in which τὸ ὑπὲρ ὑμῶν διδόμενον already followed the saying 'This is my body'. But a point
to be considered, as we shall find in several narratives in the story
of the Passion, is that Luke appears to be influenced to some
degree by the opening words in parallel Markan narratives.[3] In
the present case a motive may be suggested which is very speculative, but nonetheless may be relevant. After drawing xxii. 14–
18 from his special source, Luke may have felt himself precluded
from using the Markan narrative of the Institution (xiv. 22–5)
because he had already a parallel to Mk. xiv. 25 in Lk. xxii. 18,
and at the same time have been attracted by the substance of the
pre-Lukan source, especially if it was used in public worship at
Antioch, to which city, according to ancient tradition, he
himself belonged.[4] Imaginative construction of this kind has its
place in historical studies, but it is better to solve literary
problems by our increasing knowledge of Luke's methods, or if

[1] *Der Einsetzungsbericht*, pp. 64–80.
[2] *The Eucharistic Words of Jesus*, p. 155.
[3] Cf. Lk. xxii. 47; xxiii. 26; xxiv. 1–3. See above, p. 33.
[4] Cf. Creed, *St Luke*, p. xxi.

necessary to leave them open. The origin of 20*b*, we have seen, is one of these questions, and all that we are able to say is that probably it stood in the pre-Lukan source and is non-Markan.

The age of the pre-Lukan source

For our present purpose it is not necessary to discuss this question in detail. Schürmann describes the source as 'the original account' (*Urbericht*) of the Eucharist and prints a Greek text in the form in which he thinks it was current.[1] Jeremias prefers to think that Mk. xiv. 22–5 is the oldest text, and supports his claim by pointing out no less than twenty-three Semitisms in it.[2] In his third edition, however, he says that in a letter dated 25 March 1959, Schürmann says he would no longer employ the term *Urbericht* for the pre-Lukan source in Lk. xxii. 19f., and Jeremias himself admits that the exact form of the tradition cannot be reconstructed, while maintaining that Mk. xiv. 22–5 stands nearest to it.[3] The opinion may be hazarded that it is mistaken to assume the existence of a primitive source from which all the New Testament narratives are derived. It is probable that various centres in early Christianity, Jerusalem, Caesarea, and Antioch, each had its own account for use in public worship and that in varying degrees one influenced another. The difference between 'my blood of the covenant' (Mk. xiv. 24) and 'the new covenant in my blood' (Lk. xxii. 20 and 1 Cor. xi. 25) may be a case in point, since Mark's phrase was liable to cause offence in the eyes of some Jewish Christians. The broad conclusion emerges that the eucharistic narratives are very early indeed and closely reflect what Jesus actually said. Their theological importance is very considerable since they suggest that the thought of Jesus was influenced by Exod. xxiv. 8, Isa. liii, and Jer. xxxi. 31ff., and that he spoke to his disciples at the Last Supper of his atoning death for men.

---

[1] *Der Einsetzungsbericht*, pp. 130f., καὶ λαβὼν ἄρτον εὐχαριστήσας (εὐλογήσας ?) ἔκλασεν καὶ ἔδωκεν αὐτοῖς καὶ εἶπεν· (λάβετε· ?) τοῦτό ἐστιν τὸ σῶμά μου τὸ ὑπὲρ ὑμῶν διδόμενον· τοῦτο ποιεῖτε εἰς τὴν ἐμὴν ἀνάμνησιν. ὡσαύτως καὶ τὸ ποτήριον μετὰ τὸ δειπνῆσαι, λέγων· τοῦτο τὸ ποτήριον ἡ καινὴ διαθήκη ἐν τῷ αἵματί μου.

[2] *The Eucharistic Words of Jesus*, pp. 173–84.

[3] *Op. cit.* pp. 190f.

5. THE PREDICTION OF THE BETRAYAL

(Lk. xxii. 21–3; cf. Mk. xiv. 18–21; Matt. xxvi. 21–5)

[21] Πλὴν ἰδοὺ ἡ χεὶρ τοῦ παραδιδόντος με μετ' ἐμοῦ ἐπὶ τῆς τραπέζης. [22] ὅτι ὁ υἱὸς μὲν τοῦ ἀνθρώπου κατὰ τὸ ὡρισμένον πορεύεται, πλὴν οὐαὶ τῷ ἀνθρώπῳ ἐκείνῳ δι' οὗ παραδίδοται. [23] καὶ αὐτοὶ ἤρξαντο συζητεῖν πρὸς ἑαυτοὺς τὸ τίς ἄρα εἴη ἐξ αὐτῶν ὁ τοῦτο μέλλων πράσσειν.

In this narrative of forty-six words, eighteen (39.1 per cent) are common to Luke and Mark. Of these thirteen are in verse 22. The question is therefore raised whether this verse is a Markan insertion in a non-Markan narrative.

In discussing the origin of this narrative, Schürmann[1] and Rehkopf[2] take opposite views. Both rely on linguistic and stylistic arguments, but whereas Schürmann maintains the Markan origin of the narrative, Rehkopf holds that it is entirely non-Markan. This disagreement suggests that it is not enough to depend on linguistic arguments alone. Other phenomena, including the distribution of 'common words', need also to be taken into account. Consideration also needs to be given to the principle adopted by Jeremias that deviations in order must 'be regarded as indications that Luke is not following Mark'.[3] In Mark the narrative precedes the account of the Supper; in Luke it follows that account.

On the linguistic side Rehkopf's case is the stronger. In favour of the pre-Lukan origin of verse 21 he cites the substitution of πλήν for ἀμὴν λέγω ὑμῖν, the Semitic use of ἰδού without a copula, the use of χείρ to describe the traitor, and of the present participle παραδιδόντος used in a future sense. He reaches the same conclusion in respect of verse 23, maintaining that the agreement with Mark in the use of ἤρξαντο is too weak a support for affirming dependence, and claiming that συζητεῖν πρὸς ἑαυτούς points to a pre-Lukan source. He points out that Luke's hand is visible in the characteristic use of τό to introduce an indirect question, the presence of the optative εἴη, and of ἄρα,

---

[1] *Jesu Abschiedsrede*, pp. 3–21.   [2] *LS*, pp. 7–30.
[3] *The Eucharistic Words of Jesus*, p. 98.

καὶ αὐτοί, μέλλων, and πράσσειν. His view of verse 22 is less convincing. He instances the unusual position of μέν, and possible translation-variants in πορεύεται/ὑπάγει, κατὰ τὸ ὡρισμένον/ καθὼς γέγραπται περὶ αὐτοῦ, and πλήν/δέ as different settings of an Aramaic word of the Lord. This view of verse 22 may be right, but the alternative possibility that it is a Markan insertion seems preferable, especially when 72 per cent of its words are common to Luke and Mark.

Rehkopf strengthens his argument by comparing the four accounts of the incident in the gospels. In Mark the disciples press for a closer indication of the traitor, asking 'Is it I?', but get no answer save that he is one of the Twelve. In Matt., Judas himself asks 'Is it I, Rabbi?', and receives the reply, 'You have said so.' In John the Beloved Disciple secretly asks, 'Lord, who is it?', and receives the answer, 'It is he to whom I shall give this morsel when I have dipped it.' Jesus then dips the morsel, gives it to Judas and says, 'What you are going to do, do quickly.' The evangelist says that Satan entered into him, that the other disciples did not know what Jesus meant, and ends his account with the dramatic statement, 'So having received the morsel, he immediately went out; and it was night' (Jn. xiii. 25–30).

In contrast with these narratives, the Lukan account is the most primitive. No question about the traitor is addressed to Jesus, but the disciples merely discuss among themselves who he might be. It is clear that the narrative stands at the beginning o a development in the tradition arising from a sense of offence at the presence of Judas at the Supper.

Schürmann traces verse 22 to Mark, but his claim that 21 and 23 are also Markan is difficult to accept. He does not recognise that all the fourteen or fifteen instances of πλήν are in L and his interpretation of the absence of ἀμὴν λέγω ὑμῖν from the versef is doubtful. Of thirteen Markan passages which contain the phrase seven have parallels in Luke. In three of these Luke takes over the phrase, and in the remaining four, while ἀμήν is omitted, λέγω ὑμῖν (σοι) is allowed to stand. Lk. xxii. 21 is the only passage in which the whole expression is wanting. These facts support Rehkopf's claim. Even less convincing is Schürmann's explanation of verse 23. He argues that the numerous Lukan words in the verse suggest that Luke is editing Mark, but it is equally possible that he is editing a non-Markan source, and this alternative is supported by the fact that ἤρξαντο is the only word out of fifteen common to Luke and Mark.

Summary

We conclude that the narrative is non-Markan and that probably verse 22 is a Markan insertion. This is the view advocated in *BTG*, pp. 4of. Simple in structure and content, the account appears to antedate the narratives of Mark, Matt., and John.

6. THE DISCOURSE ON TRUE GREATNESS AND THE SAYING ABOUT TWELVE THRONES

(Lk. xxii. 24–30; cf. Mk. x. 42–5;
Matt. xx. 25–8 and xix. 28)

[24] Ἐγένετο δὲ καὶ φιλονεικία ἐν αὐτοῖς, τὸ τίς αὐτῶν δοκεῖ εἶναι μείζων. [25] ὁ δὲ εἶπεν <u>αὐτοῖς· οἱ βασιλεῖς τῶν ἐθνῶν κυριεύου-</u> <u>σιν αὐτῶν, καὶ οἱ ἐξουσιάζοντες αὐτῶν</u> εὐεργέται καλοῦνται· [26] <u>ὑμεῖς δὲ οὐχ οὕτως, ἀλλ’ ὁ μείζων ἐν ὑμῖν γινέσθω ὡς ὁ</u> <u>νεώτερος, καὶ ὁ ἡγούμενος ὡς ὁ διακονῶν.</u> [27] τίς γὰρ μείζων, ὁ ἀνακείμενος ἢ ὁ διακονῶν; οὐχὶ ὁ ἀνακείμενος; ἐγὼ δὲ ἐν μέσῳ ὑμῶν εἰμι ὡς ὁ διακονῶν.

[28] <u>ὑμεῖς δέ ἐστε οἱ διαμεμενηκότες μετ’ ἐμοῦ ἐν τοῖς πειρασμοῖς μου</u> [29] <u>κἀγὼ διατίθεμαι ὑμῖν καθὼς διέθετό μοι ὁ πατήρ μου</u> <u>βασιλείαν,</u> [30] <u>ἵνα ἔσθητε καὶ πίνητε ἐπὶ τῆς τραπέζης μου ἐν τῇ</u> <u>βασιλείᾳ μου, καὶ καθήσεσθε ἐπὶ θρόνων κρίνοντες τὰς δώδεκα</u> <u>φυλὰς τοῦ Ἰσραήλ.</u>

Note. In verses 24–7 the words common to Luke and Mark are underlined, and in 28–30 (not in Mark) those common to Luke and Matt.

Lk. xxii. 24–30 consists of a discourse in verses 24–7 and a saying in verses 28–30. Whether the saying on twelve thrones originally belonged to 24–7 is uncertain. It has often been assigned to Q, but in view of the differences between it and the parallel version in Matt. xix. 28, Streeter included the latter in M and the Lukan version in L.[1] Otto maintained that in the primitive account it

---

[1] *FG*, p. 288.

followed Lk. xxii. 19*a*.[1] Schürmann argues that it is highly probable that Lk. xxii. 28–30 was immediately connected with Lk. xxii. 15–20*a*, and that subsequently Lk. xxii. 24–7 was inserted in this complex, verse 27 being a separate unit of tradition.[2] These suggestions are speculative. More important is the claim that Lk. xxii. 24–7 was derived, not from Mk. x. 41–5, the story of the ambitious request of James and John, but from pre-Lukan non-Markan tradition.[3] This hypothesis is based on a very detailed linguistic examination of the two narratives. Numerical considerations, arising from the presence of 'common' words, are not neglected, but Schürmann's arguments are almost exclusively linguistic. In *BTG*, pp. 41f., greater importance was given to the numerical argument. It was pointed out that twenty-one of the sixty-seven words of the narrative are shared by Luke and Mark (31 per cent), a proportion not unduly high when it is remembered that independent versions must have much in common, and that verses 24, 26*b*, and 27 owe little, if anything, to Mark. This argument is strengthened by the difference in time and circumstance. 'It is not easy', I wrote, 'to think that Luke would cut out a passage from a different narrative and thrust it into an entirely new context. Such does not appear to have been his habit where Mark is concerned.'[4] I have already mentioned the claim of Jeremias that deviations in order indicate that Luke is not following Mark.[5] Schürmann also denies that Luke changes the position of single narratives and points out that he introduces the few exceptions to this rule as soon as possible in the immediate vicinity, not many chapters later.[6]

These arguments are supported by the linguistic character of Lk. xxii. 24–30. The facts are best displayed in a linguistic commentary.

Verse 24

In this verse there are no words common to Mark's narrative. Characteristic of Luke are ἐγένετο, δὲ καί, and τὸ τίς. φιλονεικία appears here only in the New Testament. Schürmann notes that forms of μείζων (three times in this narrative) are wanting in

---

[1] *The Kingdom of God and the Son of Man*, p. 316.
[2] *Jesu Abschiedsrede*, pp. 54–63.
[3] *Op. cit.* pp. 65–92.   [4] *BTG*, p. 42.   [5] See above, p. 59.
[6] *Jesu Abschiedsrede*, p. 64, 'Luk kennt keine Umstellung vom Einzelperikopen.'

Acts and are found in Luke only when a source is being used (Q in vii. 28; Mark in ix. 46; L in xii. 18). He suggests that Luke composed this introductory verse or, more probably, is editing a non-Markan source.

Verses 25–6

In 25–6a fourteen or fifteen words are common to Mark. On the other hand εἶπεν c. dat. is much less frequent in Luke than εἶπεν πρός c. acc. and is claimed by Rehkopf as pre-Lukan. βασιλεύς appears in Luke ten times and twenty times in Acts. The simplex κυριεύουσιν is unusual if Luke is copying Mark who has κατα-κυριεύουσιν. So also is ἐξουσιάζω, a verb which as a designation of rank is not used by him elsewhere. On the other hand he often has the adjectival participle. εὐεργέτης is found in the New Testament here only, but Luke uses καλέω in the sense of 'to name' relatively often. Schürmann describes Luke's ὑμεῖς δὲ οὐχ οὕτως as a smoother rendering than Mark's οὐχ οὕτως δέ ἐστιν ἐν ὑμῖν, but doubts if Luke would have altered it of himself. Neither νεώτερος (xv. 12f.; Acts v. 6*) nor ἡγούμενος* is distinctive of Luke, but may reflect community speech. On the whole Schürmann concludes that Mk. x. 41–4 is more original than Lk. xxii. 24–6, which he describes as an edited version standing near to Matt. xxiii. 11. It is of interest to recall that J. M. Creed, who maintains that the Lukan Passion narrative is based on Mark, admits that the differences of wording and thought make it probable that Luke is here dependent on a non-Markan source.[1]

Verse 27

The only word common to Luke and Mark is διακονεῖν. Schürmann subjects the saying to meticulous comparison with Mk. x. 45 (the 'ransom saying') word by word and phrase by phrase.[2] He denies that the saying is an edited version of Mk. x. 45 and suggests that, like Lk. xxii. 24–6, it is based on a pre-Markan source. It is impossible to record here his closely reasoned argument which extends to thirteen pages and includes a powerful defence of the originality of Mk. x. 45. Among other things he points out that of himself Luke nowhere uses ἀνακεῖσ-θαι, but has ἐν μέσῳ c. gen. relatively frequently.

---

[1] *St Luke*, p. 267.
[2] *Jesu Abschiedsrede*, pp. 80–92.

Verses 28–30

There can be little doubt that the saying on 'twelve thrones' is derived from a source independent of Matt. xix. 28. The latter is affected by its Markan context. This is visible in οἱ ἀκολουθήσαντές μοι (cf. Mk. x. 28). The reference to the Son of Man seated on the throne of his glory has the imagery of Matt. xxv. 31, and ἐν τῇ παλινγενεσίᾳ, which has no Semitic equivalent,[1] reveals the hand of Matthew. Redaction in the Lukan version is less apparent. διαμένω (Lk. i. 22*) is rare in Luke, although πειρασμός appears several times. 'In my temptations' may have meant Satanic snares in Q, but Luke seems to be using the phrase with reference to the earthly life of Jesus. There is no parallel in Matt. to Luke's 'But now I vest in you the kingship which my Father vested in me' (NEB), but the promise follows well if the words were spoken at the Supper (cf. the references to a Covenant in Lk. xxii. 20 and Mk. xiv. 24). In the L source there are several references to the Messianic Feast (Lk. xiv. 15; xxii. 16, 18), and its language may well be retained in ἵνα *c. subj.*, since Luke often prefers the infinitive.[2] The absence of δώδεκα in the phrase ἐπὶ θρόνων may be editorial in view of the reference to the betrayal in Lk. xxii. 21–3. B is probably right in reading τὰς δώδεκα φυλάς before κρίνοντες, the alternative reading being an assimilation to the text of Matt. T. W. Manson[3] agrees with Streeter in assigning the Matthaean form to M and the Lukan parallel to L.

Summary

The conclusion is justified that Lk. xxii. 24–7 is derived from a non-Markan source and that both this narrative and the saying on 'twelve thrones' belonged to the L source. With reference to the narrative Easton says, 'Direct dependence on Mk is too difficult an hypothesis, especially in view of Lk's position for the saying.'[4] Of verses 28–30 he says that its derivation from Q is quite uncertain.

[1] Cf. Dalman, *The Words of Jesus*, p. 177.
[2] Cf. Cadbury, *The Style and Literary Method of Luke*, pp. 137f.
[3] *SJ*, p. 216.
[4] *St Luke*, p. 324. Of Lk. xxii. 24–7 C. H. Dodd writes, 'It would be rash to conclude that Luke is here copying from Mark', *HTFG*, p. 61.

7. THE EXHORTATION TO SIMON

(Lk. xxii. 31–4; cf. Mk. xiv. 29–30; Matt. xxvi. 33–4)

[31] Σίμων Σίμων, ἰδοὺ ὁ σατανᾶς ἐξητήσατο ὑμᾶς τοῦ σινιάσαι ὡς τὸν σῖτον· [32] ἐγὼ δὲ ἐδεήθην περὶ σοῦ, ἵνα μὴ ἐκλίπῃ ἡ πίστις σου· καὶ σύ ποτε ἐπιστρέψας στήρισον τοὺς ἀδελφούς σου. [33] ὁ δὲ εἶπεν αὐτῷ· κύριε, μετὰ σοῦ ἕτοιμός εἰμι καὶ εἰς φυλακὴν καὶ εἰς θάνατον πορεύεσθαι. [34] ὁ δὲ εἶπεν· λέγω σοι, Πέτρε, οὐ φωνήσει σήμερον ἀλέκτωρ ἕως τρίς με ἀπαρνήσῃ εἰδέναι.

The narrative is peculiar to Luke and, with the exception of verse 34, is derived from Luke's special source L. There are signs of Luke's hand, but more linguistic indications that he is using a pre-Lukan source. τοῦ *c. infin.* and δέομαι are characteristic of him,[1] and other words are frequently found in Luke/Acts. These include πορεύομαι, ἰδού, φυλακή, ἕτοιμος,[2] and ἐπιστρέφειν. ἐξαιτέομαι and σινιάζειν occur here only in the New Testament, and ποτέ here only in Luke/Acts. The words included in Rehkopf's list of pre-Lukan expressions[3] are the vocatives Σίμων Σίμων and κύριε, together with σατανᾶς, ἐκλείπειν, στηρίζειν, εἶπεν *c. dat.*, and ἕως.

The non-Markan origin of 31f. is obvious, the only question being whether it is a definite unit in itself. Its theme is the defection and restoration of Simon, but it contains no express reference to the denial, although it prepares the way for it.[4]

Verse 34 is probably a Markan addition[5] based on Mk. xiv. 29f. Half its words (8/15) are common to Luke and Mark. It explicitly alludes to the denial, and it is significant that the narrative of the denial itself is also Markan.[6] It has often been pointed out that, whereas 31 is addressed to 'Simon', this verse has the vocative 'Peter'. These features stamp 34 as of a different coinage from 31–3.

Schürmann[7] claims verse 33 as also Markan, but this claim can hardly be sustained. Only three words (out of sixteen) are

---

[1] Cf. Hawkins, *Horae Synopticae*, pp. 16–23.
[2] Cf. Acts xxiii. 15.   [3] *LS*, pp. 91–9.
[4] See below, p. 78.   [5] Cf. T. W. Manson, *SJ*, p. 339.
[6] Nearly half its words are common to Luke and Mark. See below, p. 77.
[7] *Jesu Abschiedsrede*, pp. 27–35. Cf. J. M. Creed, *St Luke*, p. 269.

common to Luke and Mark (ὁ δέ and αὐτῷ) and these are not significant. It is possible that 33 might be explained as editorial, devised by Luke to prepare the way for the Markan addition in 34; there is, for example, a parallel in Acts xxiii. 15 in the words ἕτοιμοί ἐσμεν τοῦ ἀνελεῖν αὐτόν. But if this were so we should expect πρός *c. acc.* after εἶπεν, and σύν instead of μετά. Moreover, 33 agrees well in thought with 31f. It is natural that after the prophecy of his defection Peter should express his devotion boldly, and declare his resolution to face prison and death with Jesus. The presumption is that the whole of 31–3 is non-Markan.[1]

Several scholars have referred to Old Testament passages in the Septuagint which are reflected in 31–3. The most obvious are the Prologue to the book of Job and Zech. iii. 1ff. in which Satan is the accuser, whose function it is to reveal the faults of men. This idea appears in 31 in the words, 'Simon, Simon, behold Satan asked to have you, that he might sift you as wheat.' In 32 Jesus is the advocate who intercedes for Peter and the rest. A second example, mentioned by W. K. L. Clarke,[2] is 2 Sam. xv. 20f., which contains striking verbal parallels with 32f. Consider the list: ἐπιστρέφου, καί, τοὺς ἀδελφούς σου, εἶπεν, κύριος, εἰς θάνατον, καί, εἰς, which might seem to be taken from the Lukan passage. Actually the list is taken from 2 Sam. xv. 20f. The experience of David is in mind during his flight from Absalom. This use of the Septuagint is characteristic of Luke. To this extent it points to him as the author of the narrative or, alternatively, to the unknown author of the L source. The implied allusion to David is one of the more reputable examples of typology.

Summary

We conclude that Lk. xxii. 31–3 is of non-Markan origin and that verse 34 is a later Markan addition to the narrative.

8. THEN AND NOW

(Lk. xxii. 35–8)

[35] Καὶ εἶπεν αὐτοῖς· ὅτε ἀπέστειλα ὑμᾶς ἄτερ βαλλαντίου καὶ πήρας καὶ ὑποδημάτων, μή τινος ὑστερήσατε; οἱ δὲ εἶπαν·

---

[1] Cf. *BTG*, pp. 42f.; P. Winter, *NTS*, IV (1958), 225.

[2] *BC*, II, 104. Cf. J. M. Creed, *St Luke*, p. 269; H. Schürmann, *Jesu Abschiedsrede*, p. 32.

οὐθενός. [36] εἶπεν δὲ αὐτοῖς· ἀλλὰ νῦν ὁ ἔχων βαλλάντιον ἀράτω, ὁμοίως καὶ πήραν, καὶ ὁ μὴ ἔχων πωλησάτω τὸ ἱμάτιον αὐτοῦ καὶ ἀγορασάτω μάχαιραν. [37] λέγω γὰρ ὑμῖν ὅτι τοῦτο τὸ γεγραμμένον δεῖ τελεσθῆναι ἐν ἐμοί, τό· καὶ μετὰ ἀνόμων ἐλογίσθη· καὶ γὰρ τὸ περὶ ἐμοῦ τέλος ἔχει. [38] οἱ δὲ εἶπαν· κύριε, ἰδοὺ μάχαιραι ὧδε δύο. ὁ δὲ εἶπεν αὐτοῖς· ἱκανόν ἐστιν.

This narrative is wholly peculiar to Luke. The references to 'purse', 'wallet', and 'shoes' point back to the mission of the Seventy (Lk. x. 4), and are meant to throw into relief the very different situation which now confronts the disciples. During the mission they could count on a friendly reception and ready hospitality, but not so now. The saying in verse 36 is ironical. '"It is different now," he said; "whoever has a purse had better take it with him, and his pack too; and if he has no sword, let him sell his cloak to buy one"' (NEB). 'This short dialogue', writes T. W. Manson, 'throws a brilliant light on the tragedy of the Ministry...The grim irony of v. 36 is the utterance of a broken heart.'[1] Jesus knows that his approaching death is certain. That is why he quotes what the prophet had said of the Servant of the Lord, 'And he was counted among the outlaws', a prophecy, he believes, which must be fulfilled in himself. The phrase καὶ γὰρ τὸ περὶ ἐμοῦ τέλος ἔχει is well translated by Klostermann,[2] 'For my life draws to its end.' The disciples misunderstand Jesus and take his words literally. They imagine he is speaking of armed resistance and cry, 'Lord, behold here are two swords.' In tones of the deepest sadness Jesus breaks off the conversation, crying, 'It is enough.' Burkitt was fully justified in observing not only that the section is one which contains some of 'the saddest words in the Gospels', but also that the mournful irony with which they are pervaded seems to him 'wholly alien from the kind of utterance which a Christian Evangelist would invent for his Master'.[3]

The claim that the narrative is derived from a source is strongly sustained by the linguistic phenomena. There is a notable absence of words and phrases characteristic of Luke. τὸ περὶ ἐμοῦ and ὁμοίως are the only two in Hawkins's list, apart from

---

[1] SJ, p. 341.
[2] Das Lukasevangelium, p. 214.
[3] The Gospel History and its Transmission, pp. 140f.

5-2

particles which are not peculiar to him. Moreover, ten of eleven examples of ὁμοίως belong to the L source, and so are claimed by Rehkopf as pre-Lukan. Rehkopf's harvest includes: βαλλάντιον, ὑπόδημα, εἶπεν c. dat. (three times), ὁμοίως, λέγω γὰρ ὑμῖν, καὶ γάρ, and κύριε. Negatively and positively these facts make derivation from L reasonably certain.

The narrative is a fitting close to the section Lk. xxii. 14–38, which several scholars have recognised as a unit in a pre-Lukan Passion narrative supplemented by additions from Mark. Schürmann strongly supports this view by his linguistic analysis. His suggestion that at one time xxii. 28–30 immediately followed xxii. 20a is mentioned above, p. 62.

Summary

We conclude that xxii. 35–8 is derived from a pre-Lukan source and that it is only lightly edited by Luke. This conclusion applies to xxii. 14–38 as a whole with the exception of verses 22 and 34, which were probably added by the evangelist in the process of compiling the Gospel. Whether the history of the section can be carried further back is an interesting question which cannot be decisively answered. But there can be no objection in principle to the possibility that originally 28–30 followed 20, if the originality of 19b–20 is accepted. In this case, as Schürmann suggests, (21–3 and) 24–7 may have been subsequently inserted, and 31–2 (3) and 35–8 added under the influence of Johannine tradition regarding conversations after the Supper.[1] We must distinguish, however, between these highly speculative suggestions and the more certain hypothesis that 14–38, less the Markan additions mentioned above, is a pre-Lukan unit.[2]

---

[1] Cf. the somewhat different reconstruction of W. L. Knox, who maintains that the Markan Passion story is a compilation of two sources, a Disciples' source and a Twelve-source; *The Sources of the Synoptic Gospels*, I, 116–47. Unfortunately Knox does not discuss the Lukan Passion story. Of Lk. xxii. 35–8, C. H. Dodd writes, 'This comes clearly from some non-Markan source'; *HTFG*, p. 51.

[2] In the light of the discussion on pp. 47–58 above, it would seem that verses 19–20, as well as the 'Markan additions' in verses 22 and 34, should be excluded from the 'pre-Lukan unit' of xxii. 14–38 referred to in the foregoing paragraph. See above, pp. 57f., where verses 19–20 are ascribed to 'a pre-Lukan liturgical source' distinct from L [Ed.].

9. THE AGONY

(Lk. xxii. 39–46; cf. Mk. xiv. 26, 32–8;
Matt. xxvi. 30, 36–41)

[39] Καὶ ἐξελθὼν ἐπορεύθη κατὰ τὸ ἔθος εἰς τὸ ὄρος τῶν ἐλαιῶν· ἠκολούθησαν δὲ αὐτῷ καὶ οἱ μαθηταί. [40] γενόμενος δὲ ἐπὶ τοῦ τόπου εἶπεν αὐτοῖς· προσεύχεσθε μὴ εἰσελθεῖν εἰς πειρασμόν. [41] καὶ αὐτὸς ἀπεσπάσθη ἀπ' αὐτῶν ὡσεὶ λίθου βολήν, καὶ θεὶς τὰ γόνατα προσηύχετο [42] λέγων· πάτερ, εἰ βούλει παρένεγκε τοῦτο τὸ ποτήριον ἀπ' ἐμοῦ· πλὴν μὴ τὸ θέλημά μου ἀλλὰ τὸ σὸν γινέσθω. [[43] ὤφθη δὲ αὐτῷ ἄγγελος ἀπ' οὐρανοῦ ἐνισχύων αὐτόν. [44] καὶ γενόμενος ἐν ἀγωνίᾳ ἐκτενέστερον προσηύχετο· καὶ ἐγένετο ὁ ἱδρὼς αὐτοῦ ὡσεὶ θρόμβοι αἵματος καταβαίνοντες ἐπὶ τὴν γῆν.] [45] καὶ ἀναστὰς ἀπὸ τῆς προσευχῆς, ἐλθὼν πρὸς τοὺς μαθητὰς εὗρεν κοιμωμένους αὐτοὺς ἀπὸ τῆς λύπης, [46] καὶ εἶπεν αὐτοῖς· τί καθεύδετε; ἀναστάντες προσεύχεσθε, ἵνα μὴ εἰσέλθητε εἰς πειρασμόν.

The percentage of common words is 26. If we exclude verses 43f., which are omitted by important MSS, it rises to 34 per cent. It is, doubtful, however, whether we ought to exclude these verses, for their omission is more easy to explain than their later insertion.[1] In any case the percentage is low and it raises a serious doubt that Luke's source is Mk. xiv. 26, 32–8. The only continuous passage common to Luke and Mark is 46*b*, 'Pray that you enter not into temptation.' It is possible that this passage is a Markan addition, since Luke has the same saying in 40.

A comparison of the two narratives strongly supports the independence of Luke's account. In Luke there is no reference to the name 'Gethsemane'; the scene is described, as in Jn. xviii. 2, as 'the place' (τόπος).[2] Luke makes no reference to the separation of Peter, James, and John from the rest. He does not describe Jesus as 'greatly amazed and sore troubled', nor does he record the saying, 'My soul is exceeding sorrowful even unto death.' In Luke, Jesus withdraws from his disciples 'a stone's cast'; in

---

[1] Cf. V. Taylor, *The Text of the New Testament*, pp. 93f.
[2] Mark has χωρίον.

Mark, having separated the three from the rest, he goes forward a little and falls to the ground. In Luke he kneels. Apart from the words, 'Remove this cup from me', which might be expected in any account of the incident, the two versions of the prayer differ in phraseology. Later Jesus addresses all the disciples; in Mark, Peter and then the rest. To the remainder of the Markan story Luke has no parallel – the reproach addressed to Peter, the saying, 'The spirit is willing, but the flesh is weak', the threefold prayer and the threefold reference to the sleeping disciples, the saying, 'It is enough: the hour is come', and the words about the approach of Judas. Some of these differences are small, and no-one would lay much stress upon them, but taken together they support the view that Luke's version is independent of Mark. The doubtful point is whether 46b is a Markan pendant.

The linguistic features of the narrative are remarkable and of great interest in their suggestiveness. The words and phrases listed by Rehkopf are comparatively few in number: κατὰ τὸ ἔθος, εἶπεν αὐτοῖς (twice), πάτερ, and πλήν. In this respect, as we shall see in a later section, the narrative differs from the account of the arrest which follows. The characteristic Lukan words are also few: ἔθος, καὶ αὐτός, ὡσεί (twice), and ἀναστάς (twice),[1] but here it is to be noted that some of Luke's words and phrases, though rare in the New Testament, are found mainly in Acts. These include θεὶς τὰ γόνατα (here and Acts vii. 60; ix. 40; xx. 36; xxi. 5; and Mk. xv. 19**), ἐνισχύω (Acts ix. 19**), ἐκτενῶς (Acts xii. 5; 1 Pet. i. 22**), ἀποσπάω (Acts xx. 30; xxi. 1; Matt. xxvi. 51**). Along with these linguistic facts two broader considerations should be borne in mind: (a) that Lk. xxii. 14–38 may at one time have existed as an independent unit, and (b) that at a very early stage the Passion story began with the arrest of Jesus.[2] The possibility is suggested that Lk. xxii. 39–46 was composed by Luke himself on the basis of earlier tradition in order to connect xxii. 14–38 with xxii. 47ff., that is, the story of the Supper with that of the arrest. This is conjecture, but it is supported by the fact that 'while he was still speaking' in verse 47 refers to different sayings in Luke and Mark; in Luke to the exhortation 'Rise and pray'; in Mark to the

---

[1] πλήν is in Hawkins's list, but it is characteristic of the L source.
[2] Cf. Jeremias, *The Eucharistic Words of Jesus*, p. 94 and Bultmann, *Die Geschichte der synoptischen Tradition*, p. 302 (English translation, p. 279).

reference to the arrival of the traitor, 'Arise, let us be going: behold, he that betrays me is at hand' (Mk. xiv. 41f.). Is the difference due to the Lukan account of the action of Judas in xxii. 47–53? This suggestion, for what it is worth, would account for the presence of two similar sayings about prayer to be delivered from testing (verses 40 and 46). Luke appears deliberately to avoid the threefold account of the coming of Jesus to the sleeping disciples in Mk. xiv. 37ff.

Several considerations suggest that at one time the Passion story began with the arrest. (1) John and Mark vary considerably in the order of events before the arrest, but from this point onwards they agree closely. (2) The third prophecy of the Passion in Mk. x. 33 begins with the handing over of Jesus to the Jewish authorities (cf. ix. 31). This fact is usually accounted for by the influence of the Passion story on the detailed saying,[1] but it may reflect a common tradition. (3) Judas is mentioned in the accounts of the arrest as if for the first time ('the man called Judas, one of the Twelve', Lk. xxii. 47a, cf. Mk. xiv. 43). (4) Both Mk. xiv. 32 and Lk. xxii. 45 describe the disciples as οἱ μαθηταί in the story of Gethsemane, but later as οἱ παρεστηκότες (Mk. xiv. 47), πάντες (Mk. xiv. 50), οἱ περὶ αὐτόν (Lk. xxii. 49), never again as οἱ μαθηταί, although this name is very common elsewhere.[2]

Summary

All the facts suggest that Lk. xxii. 39–46 is non-Markan in origin, with the possibility that verse 46b is a Markan addition to the narrative.[3]

This conclusion must be distinguished from the more speculative suggestion that the narrative was used by the evangelist to connect the stories of the Last Supper and the arrest. The vocabulary does not favour the view that it is a free composition on the part of Luke;[4] it is better explained as the Lukan embel-

[1] Cf. Taylor, St Mark, p. 436.
[2] Jeremias, The Eucharistic Words of Jesus, pp. 94f.
[3] BTG, pp. 43–5.
[4] Lukan elements in the narrative are not sufficiently numerous to point to Luke's authorship, while non-Lukan elements persist. C. H. Dodd writes, 'In short, there is no sufficient reason to believe that Luke used Mark at all in this section (Lk. xxii. 40–6) (for the two clauses common to both are such as would be likely to occur even in independent forms of the tradition)', HTFG, p. 66.

lishment of a pre-Lukan source, oral or written. The narrative has a primitive ring. Vv. 43f. reflect an early period when it was natural to dwell upon the sufferings of Christ. It is less likely to have been added at a later time and its early omission can be readily understood.[1]

10. THE ARREST

(Lk. xxii. 47–54a; cf. Mk. xiv. 43–52;
Matt. xxvi. 47–56)

[47] Ἔτι αὐτοῦ λαλοῦντος, ἰδοὺ ὄχλος καὶ ὁ λεγόμενος Ἰούδας εἷς τῶν δώδεκα προήρχετο αὐτούς, καὶ ἤγγισεν τῷ Ἰησοῦ φιλῆσαι αὐτόν. [48] Ἰησοῦς δὲ εἶπεν αὐτῷ· Ἰούδα, φιλήματι τὸν υἱὸν τοῦ ἀνθρώπου παραδίδως; [49] ἰδόντες δὲ οἱ περὶ αὐτὸν τὸ ἐσόμενον εἶπαν· κύριε, εἰ πατάξομεν ἐν μαχαίρῃ; [50] καὶ ἐπάταξεν εἷς τις ἐξ αὐτῶν τοῦ ἀρχιερέως τὸν δοῦλον καὶ ἀφεῖλεν τὸ οὖς αὐτοῦ τὸ δεξιόν. [51] ἀποκριθεὶς δὲ ὁ Ἰησοῦς εἶπεν· ἐᾶτε ἕως τούτου. καὶ ἁψάμενος τοῦ ὠτίου ἰάσατο αὐτόν. [52] εἶπεν δὲ Ἰησοῦς πρὸς τοὺς παραγενομένους πρὸς αὐτὸν ἀρχιερεῖς καὶ στρατηγοὺς τοῦ ἱεροῦ καὶ πρεσβυτέρους· ὡς ἐπὶ λῃστὴν ἐξεληλύθατε μετὰ μαχαιρῶν καὶ ξύλων· [53] καθ᾽ ἡμέραν ὄντος μου μεθ᾽ ὑμῶν ἐν τῷ ἱερῷ οὐκ ἐξετείνατε τὰς χεῖρας ἐπ᾽ ἐμέ. ἀλλ᾽ αὕτη ἐστὶν ὑμῶν ἡ ὥρα καὶ ἡ ἐξουσία τοῦ σκότους. [54a] συλλαβόντες δὲ αὐτὸν ἤγαγον καὶ εἰσήγαγον εἰς τὴν οἰκίαν τοῦ ἀρχιερέως.

It is manifest from the above that Luke and Mark have a considerable amount of words in common. Of the 135 words of Luke fifty-six (41.4 per cent) are present in Mark. This amount is greater than any we have yet found, but since nearly half of the words in common occur in verses 52f., the question arises

[1] On the theological significance of the Gethsemane scene, see further the treatment by R. S. Barbour, 'Gethsemane in the Tradition of the Passion', *NTS*, xvi (1970), 231ff. Barbour thinks the Lukan narrative is independent of Mark and agrees that the Gethsemane tradition 'was adopted into the Passion narrative at a fairly late stage and inserted between the story of the Last Supper (itself not an integral part of the primitive Passion narrative) and the arrest' [Ed.].

THE ARREST

whether these verses contain a Markan insertion in Luke's narrative. In *BTG* I suggested that the words καὶ ἀφεῖλεν τὸ οὖς αὐτοῦ τὸ δεξιόν in 50*b* and the passage 52–3*a* are additions to Luke's non-Markan source. I suggested that Jesus addressed 'the captains of the temple with the words, "This is your hour, and the power of darkness"'. I pointed out that Luke uses ἔτι αὐτοῦ λαλοῦντος (47*a*) more than all the other evangelists, and that the greater emphasis on the name Judas ('He that was called Judas') may be due to the fact that this is the first reference to the traitor in the Lukan Passion narrative. I observed that among other differences the multitude is mentioned first, that swords and staves are not mentioned, nor again the statement that the crowd came 'from the chief priests and the scribes and the elders'. Luke says nothing of a sign arranged by Judas to identify Jesus. He does not actually say that Judas kissed Jesus, although this is probably implied in 48, 'Judas, do you betray the Son of Man with a kiss?'[1]

This is the second of the two narratives examined by Rehkopf.[2] He examines it in the greatest detail. His results are similar to those described above, except that he takes a different view of the healing of the severed ear. They will be indicated best by considering the four parts in which he examines the narrative.

(a) The approach of the crowd (Lk. xxii. 47a)

Among the more important observations made by Rehkopf the following are noteworthy. The passage lacks a connecting particle (cf. Mark καὶ εὐθύς). Black[3] points out that asyndeton is highly characteristic of Aramaic, and Cadbury[4] observes that it is even more carefully avoided by Luke than parataxis. Further, in a Semitic manner ἰδού is used without a finite verb, and the use of ὁ λεγόμενος with 'Judas' is unusual in Luke. In view of vi. 16 one would expect 'Iscariot' to be added. Normally Luke uses ὁ καλούμενος or ὀνόματι with the names of persons, not ὁ λεγόμενος (contrast Matt.). Again nothing in the passage suggests an armed band hostile to Jesus. Finally, Rehkopf suggests, the accusative after προέρχομαι may be a 'Latinism'; the verb is usually followed by the genitive. All this mounts up to a strong

[1] *BTG*, pp. 45–7. [2] *LS*, pp. 31–82.
[3] M. Black, *An Aramaic Approach to the Gospels and Acts* (3rd ed. 1967), p. 56.
[4] *The Style and Literary Method of Luke*, p. 147.

case, indicative of the use of a source older than Mark. Nevertheless, in a short passage in which ten words (10/14) are common to both evangelists, it is difficult to resist the opinion that Luke may also be influenced by Mk. xiv. 43 (see below, p. 76).

(b) The kiss (Lk. xxii. 47b–48)

Here there are only three words in common. The simplex verb φιλεῖν is strange (Mark κατεφίλησεν), and ἐγγίζειν/προσέρχεσθαι and φιλῆσαι/κατεφίλησεν can be translation-variants. There are also material differences. Rehkopf maintains that in Luke the kiss, the treachery, and the character of Judas himself appear in another light. In Mark Judas is the crafty, cold-blooded traitor who chooses the sign of an affectionate greeting to effect the arrest: in Luke one thinks rather of a Judas who perhaps from a sudden anxiety and a still existent sense of awe is driven to the strange action of greeting Jesus with a kiss.[1] The words of Jesus are not a warning or a reproach, but an expression of grief.[2] Linguistic details in verse 48 suggest that Luke is not indulging in redactional activity, but is using a source. These include εἶπεν c. dat., the vocative 'Ιούδα, the repeated naming of Jesus, the phrase 'the Son of Man'.[3]

(c) The blow with a sword (Lk. xxii. 49–51)

The speech-usage of a source is also visible in verse 49. Rehkopf[4] instances the unusual phrase for the disciples, οἱ περὶ αὐτόν, the use of εἰ in a direct question, and the instrumental use of ἐν. So also in verses 50f. The cry ἐᾶτε ἕως τούτου is of a kind that Luke often sets aside, but that is frequent in his special source; the dialogue form is often altered in Luke;[5] the phrase εἷς τις is not necessarily taken from Mark.[6] Difficulties arise in verse 50 since ten of its sixteen words agree with Mk. xiv. 47. Rehkopf suggests that in Luke the blow is an attempt at defence, whereas in Mark it is an effort to set Jesus free,[7] and he adopts the still bolder hypothesis that Mk. xiv. 47 may be an insertion[8] (perhaps from a

---

[1] LS, p. 49.
[2] Cf. BTG, p. 47, 'His words...breathe the sadness of a deeply wounded love.'
[3] Rehkopf, LS, pp. 51–6.   [4] Op. cit. pp. 56–61.
[5] Cadbury, The Style and Literary Method of Luke, pp. 79f.
[6] Cf. Taylor, St Mark, p. 559.
[7] LS, pp. 65f.; cf. C. H. Dodd, HTFG, p. 79.   [8] Op. cit. p. 67.

written source), for here only σπᾶν, ἀφαιρεῖν, and ὠτάριον are to be found in Mark.[1] To these παίειν must be added, that is 4 out of 18 words. Arguments of this kind are rarely conclusive in themselves, since the presence of words found nowhere else in an author may be due to the subject-matter. In the present case, however, there are supporting arguments. With the recognition that Mk. xiv. 47 is an insertion, a confusion in Mark's narrative is resolved, for as it now stands αὐτοῖς in xiv. 48 appears to refer to the 'by-standers' in 47, whereas in fact the reproach is addressed to the men who had arrested Jesus (οἱ δέ, 46).[2] There is force, therefore, in Rehkopf's submission that the agreements between Mk. xiv. 47 and Lk. xxii. 50 point, not to Luke's dependence on Mark, but to the dependence of both accounts on an older source.[3] Nevertheless, the alternative and simpler suggestion made at the beginning of the section, that 'and cut off his right ear' is a Markan insertion in Luke,[4] cannot lightly be rejected. This view cannot be explained away as a modern prejudice. The healing of a severed ear is discordant with the gospel tradition as a whole. In the gospels, including John, the blind, the halt, the lame, the paralysed are healed, but there is no other example of the healing of a limb cut off from the body. E. R. Micklem's words are weighty: 'It...looks as though Lk. had conflated two traditions; (1) that of Mk., which simply records that the man's ear was cut off, and (2) a tradition which tells of the healing of the ear which had been wounded by a stroke with a sword.'[5]

(d) The reproach addressed to the authorities
(Lk. xxii. 52f.)

It is obvious that, with the exception of 53b, 'This is your hour and the power of darkness', and possibly a few words from 52a, 'And Jesus said to... the captains of the temple', the greater part of 52–3a is derived from Mk. xiv. 43, 48f. Out of thirty-eight words in this passage twenty-six are common to Mark. Moreover, it is improbable that the chief priests and the elders were present at the arrest. Rehkopf conjectures that originally 52a read εἶπεν δὲ Ἰησοῦς τοῖς ἀρχιερεῦσι καὶ στρατηγοῖς τοῦ ἱεροῦ καὶ πρεσ-

---

[1] *Op. cit.* p. 67. [2] *Op. cit.* p. 66.
[3] *Op. cit.* p. 67. [4] *BTG*, pp. 46f.
[5] *Miracles and the New Psychology*, p. 46.

βυτέροις, and that 53*b* comes from Luke's special source. He interprets 52*b*–53*a* as a Markan insertion.

Rehkopf thinks that the three groups, ἀρχιερεῖς, στρατηγοί, πρεσβύτεροι, stood in Luke's source, and mentions as characteristic of the source the renewed name of Jesus and the lack of the article before the name. Signs of Luke's editorial activity appear in πρός and παραγίνεσθαι,[1] and in the attributive position of the participle between the article and the substantive (cf. Lk. i. 1 and vii. 9). Luke's hand is also to be seen in the Markan passage 52*b*–53*a* in the incorrect use of the genitive absolute ὄντος μου and in his apparent antipathy to κρατεῖν (cf. Mark).[2] Verse 53*b*, which is a reproach directed against the authorities, reads almost like an excuse after 52*b*–53*a*. ὥρα, he maintains, is not a purely historic point of time in the sense of an opportunity at this moment, but means the hour based in the redemptive plan of God and affirmed by Jesus in Gethsemane, whose significance is the handing over of the Son of Man into the hands of sinners and the powers of Satan.[3] This concept is Johannine.[4]

Summary

From the foregoing investigation it is reasonably certain that Lk. xxii. 52*b*–53*a* is a Markan insertion in a non-Markan source. Possibly the same is true of the words 'and struck off his right ear' in 50*b*, and it may be that the opening words in 47*a* reflect Markan influence. The references to the action of Judas and to the blow with a sword are distinctive and notably different from the account in Mark. Especially is this true of the words of Jesus regarding the hour determined by God and the power of darkness in 53*b*. It is remarkable how few words and phrases characteristic of Luke appear in the narrative as compared with those which point to a source. This fact implies that he follows his special source closely.[5]

---

[1] *LS*, pp. 72f.

[2] There are only two examples, in viii. 54 (= Mk. v. 41) and xxiv. 16 (L), and four in Acts.

[3] *Op. cit.* p. 81.

[4] Cf. Jn. vii. 30; viii. 20; xii. 23, 27; xiii. 1; xvii. 1.

[5] While Rehkopf's views have been described with some fulness, the student is advised to study his *Die lukanische Sonderquelle*, and especially his list illustrative of pre-Lukan source-usage.

II. THE DENIAL

(Lk. xxii. 54*b*–61; cf. Mk. xiv. 54, 66–72;
Matt. xxvi. 58, 69–75)

[54*b*] ὁ δὲ Πέτρος ἠκολούθει μακρόθεν. [55] περιαψάντων δὲ πῦρ
ἐν μέσῳ τῆς αὐλῆς καὶ συνκαθισάντων ἐκάθητο ὁ Πέτρος μέσος
αὐτῶν. [56] ἰδοῦσα δὲ αὐτὸν παιδίσκη τις καθήμενον πρὸς τὸ φῶς
καὶ ἀτενίσασα αὐτῷ εἶπεν· καὶ οὗτος σὺν αὐτῷ ἦν. [57] ὁ δὲ
ἠρνήσατο αὐτὸν λέγων· οὐκ οἶδα αὐτόν, γύναι. [58] καὶ μετὰ
βραχὺ ἕτερος ἰδὼν αὐτὸν ἔφη· καὶ σὺ ἐξ αὐτῶν εἶ. ὁ δὲ Πέτρος ἔφη·
ἄνθρωπε, οὐκ εἰμί. [59] καὶ διαστάσης ὡσεὶ ὥρας μιᾶς ἄλλος τις
διϊσχυρίζετο λέγων· ἐπ᾽ ἀληθείας καὶ οὗτος μετ᾽ αὐτοῦ ἦν, καὶ
γὰρ Γαλιλαῖός ἐστιν. [60] εἶπεν δὲ ὁ Πέτρος· ἄνθρωπε, οὐκ οἶδα ὃ
λέγεις. καὶ παραχρῆμα ἔτι λαλοῦντος αὐτοῦ ἐφώνησεν ἀλέκτωρ,
[61] καὶ στραφεὶς ὁ κύριος ἐνέβλεψεν τῷ Πέτρῳ· καὶ ὑπεμνήσθη ὁ
Πέτρος τοῦ λόγου τοῦ κυρίου, ὡς εἶπεν αὐτῷ ὅτι πρὶν ἀλέκτορα
φωνῆσαι σήμερον ἀπαρνήσῃ με τρίς.

Note. Verse 62 is omitted by 0171 a b e ff² i l* r. It agrees exactly with
Matt. xxvi. 75*b*.

In the narrative of the denial almost half the words are common
to Luke and Mark and are evenly distributed throughout. In
both Gospels the incident takes place on the evening of the
arrest. In them its position relative to the trial varies; in Luke it
precedes the mocking and the trial, in Mark it follows both, a
difference due to the fact that Luke assigns the trial to the
following morning. Luke's source is manifestly Mark. This is
suggested, not only by the number of words in common, but in
particular by the reference to Peter following 'from afar', the
phrase πρὸς τὸ φῶς, the allusion to his Galilean origin, and
especially the passage, 'And Peter remembered the word...how
(Jesus) said to him...Before the cock crows...you will deny me
three times.' The variations can be adequately explained as
inferences from Mark or as editorial modifications based possibly
on another source, but more probably on oral tradition.

Among the more important variations may be mentioned

Luke's reference to the lighting of a fire (verse 55, cf. Jn. xviii. 18, 'for it was cold') and the reference to the interval of 'about one hour' before the final challenge. Other alterations include the absence of the reference to the departure of Peter to the porch after the first challenge, the substitution of different speakers (a man) in the second and third accusations, the omission of the references to cursing and swearing and to *two* cock-crowings (if read in Mark), and the avoiding of Mark's difficult phrase καὶ ἐπιβαλὼν ἔκλαιεν, 'And he burst into tears.' Editorial modification accounts for Luke's single narrative as compared with Mark's description of the incident in two stages.

A considerable number of words in the narrative point to Luke's editorial activity. These include characteristic words: ἄγω, a συν- compound (συνκαθίζειν), τις, ἀτενίζειν, σύν, ἕτερος, ὡσεί, παραχρῆμα, and στραφείς.[1] In addition may be mentioned two verbs which occur only in Luke and Acts: διϊσχυρίζεσθαι (here and Acts xii. 15**) and διΐστημι (here, Lk. xxiv. 51, Acts xxvii. 28**).[2] In Rehkopf's list illustrative of pre-Lukan speech-usage the following appear: three vocatives (γύναι and ἄνθρωπε (twice)), ὁ κύριος (twice), εἶπεν c. dat., μακρόθεν, and στραφείς.

Summary

The conclusion to be drawn is that Mark is Luke's source[3] and perhaps his only written source. Evidence in favour of a non-Markan source is not considerable, but it cannot be ruled out. Some knowledge of oral tradition common to Luke and John can be inferred but cannot be affirmed with much certainty. Significant of Luke's dependence on Mark is the fact that his earlier reference to the denial in xxii. 34 is also Markan. If the L source did include the tradition of the denial the evidence regarding it has almost disappeared and nothing like a complete narrative can be recovered, but ignorance of the event is not likely, and the remembrance that the Lord looked upon Peter may well be a pre-Lukan reminiscence.

[1] Rehkopf, *LS*, p. 97, includes στραφείς in his list. It is absent from Acts, is present twice in Matt. and twice in John, but seven or eight times in Luke, all from the special source.
[2] There are also four examples of the genitive absolute. One of them, ἔτι λαλοῦντος αὐτοῦ, he has three times in the Passion narrative.
[3] So Creed, *St Luke*, p. 276, Easton, *St Luke*, pp. 334f.

12. THE MOCKING

(Lk. xxii. 63–5; cf. Mk. xiv. 65; Matt. xxvi. 67–8)

Lk. xxii. 63–5

[63] Καὶ οἱ ἄνδρες οἱ συνέχοντες αὐτὸν ἐνέπαιζον αὐτῷ δέροντες, [64] καὶ περικαλύψαντες αὐτὸν ἐπηρώτων λέγοντες· προφήτευσον, τίς ἐστιν ὁ παίσας σε; [65] καὶ ἕτερα πολλὰ βλασφημοῦντες ἔλεγον εἰς αὐτόν.

Mk. xiv. 65

Καὶ ἤρξαντό τινες ἐμπτύειν αὐτῷ καὶ περικαλύπτειν αὐτοῦ τὸ πρόσωπον καὶ κολαφίζειν αὐτὸν καὶ λέγειν αὐτῷ· προφήτευσον, καὶ οἱ ὑπηρέται ῥαπίσμασιν αὐτὸν ἔλαβον.

It will be seen that Luke has six words only out of twenty-seven in common with Mark. If καὶ περικαλύπτειν αὐτοῦ τὸ πρόσωπον (Om. D a f sy[s]) is an assimilation to Luke, the number falls to four. Numerically the amount of agreement is small. Not only so, the position of the incident in the two Gospels differs. In Luke the mocking follows the denial and precedes the trial before the priests on the following morning; in Mark it follows the trial and precedes the denial. There are also differences in the contents of the two narratives. In Luke the mockers are the men who effected the arrest. In Mark they appear to be members of the court, since in contrast to them the servants (οἱ ὑπηρέται) are mentioned later. Further, in Mark Jesus is spat upon and buffetted; in Luke he is mocked and beaten. These differences are increased if we accept Streeter's interpretation of the textual evidence. He accepts the view that the reference to blindfolding in Mark is not original and that the question, 'Who is it that struck thee?', is peculiar to Luke's account.[1] The blindfolding is not mentioned in Matt., and, although the question about the striker is found in Mark in W Θ 69 579 700 *et al.*, it is not found in the best MSS,

---

[1] Cf. Streeter, *FG*, pp. 325–8; Taylor, *St Mark*, p. 571. Streeter's contrast is well known. 'In Mark the mockers spit on His face and slap Him and cry, "Play the prophet now!" In Luke they veil His eyes and then, striking Him, say, "Use your prophetic gift of second sight to tell the striker's name." Each version paints a consistent picture.'

Alexandrian and Western. But, even apart from the questions of text, the differences outweigh the resemblances in Luke and Mark.

Linguistic arguments can hardly carry us far in the case of so short a narrative, but so far as they go they suggest that Luke has composed the account on the basis of his special source. His characteristic words appear in ἀνήρ, συνέχειν, and ἕτερος. He has ἐμπαίζειν five times, of which three are in the Passion narrative, and περικαλύπτειν appears here only, Mk. xiv. 65 (?), and Heb. ix. 4**. He often replaces Mark's use of ἤρξαντο as an auxiliary verb with the infinitive,[1] but retains it in sayings and frequently, as here, makes use of participles.[2] His use of the imperfect[3] in xxii. 63–5, in contrast with the aorist in Mark, is distinctive, as the translation in *NEB* shows: 'The men who were guarding Jesus mocked at him. They beat him, they blindfolded him, and they kept asking him, "Now, prophet, who hit you? Tell us that." And so they went on heaping insults upon him.'

Summary

From the few words in common, the position given to the narrative, its distinctive character, and its vocabulary, it may be concluded that Luke's account is not an edited version of Mk. xiv. 65,[4] but represents his own rewriting of material from his special source.

13. THE TRIAL BEFORE THE PRIESTS

(Lk. xxii. 66–71; cf. Mk. xiv. 55–64;
Matt. xxvi. 59–66)

[66] Καὶ ὡς ἐγένετο ἡμέρα, συνήχθη τὸ πρεσβυτέριον τοῦ λαοῦ ἀρχιερεῖς τε καὶ γραμματεῖς, καὶ ἀπήγαγον αὐτὸν εἰς τὸ συνέδριον αὐτῶν, [67] λέγοντες· εἰ σὺ εἶ ὁ Χριστός, εἰπὸν ἡμῖν. εἶπεν δὲ αὐτοῖς· ἐὰν ὑμῖν εἴπω, οὐ μὴ πιστεύσητε· [68] ἐὰν δὲ ἐρωτήσω, οὐ μὴ ἀποκριθῆτε. [69] ἀπὸ τοῦ νῦν δὲ ἔσται ὁ υἱὸς τοῦ ἀνθρώπου

---

[1] Cf. Moulton–Howard, *A Grammar of New Testament Greek*, II, 455f.
[2] Cf. Cadbury, *The Style and Literary Method of Luke*, p. 134.
[3] Cf. Cadbury, *op. cit.* p. 160.
[4] Cf. Easton: 'Lk evidently is not based on Mk', *St Luke*, p. 336.

καθήμενος ἐκ δεξιῶν τῆς δυνάμεως τοῦ θεοῦ. [70] εἶπαν δὲ πάντες· σὺ οὖν εἶ ὁ υἱὸς τοῦ θεοῦ; ὁ δὲ πρὸς αὐτοὺς ἔφη· ὑμεῖς λέγετε ὅτι ἐγώ εἰμι. [71] οἱ δὲ εἶπαν· τί ἔτι ἔχομεν μαρτυρίας χρείαν; αὐτοὶ γὰρ ἠκούσαμεν ἀπὸ τοῦ στόματος αὐτοῦ.

Note. Verse 69 is a semi-quotation based on Dan. vii. 13 and Ps. cx. 1.

Commentators differ widely on the question of Luke's source. Creed says dependence on Mark is 'unmistakable'.[1] Easton favours the hypothesis of a special source, but says that the narrative contains reminiscences of Mark.[2] The number of 'common words' can be interpreted differently. Thirty-three out of ninety-four (35.1 per cent) appear in Luke and Mark, but they are not significant and are such as would be naturally used in references to the question of Messiahship. The difference in order and in time is more important and points to the use of a source. Mark describes the trial at night, and follows it with the mocking and the denial. Luke first relates the denial and the mocking and then records the trial on the following morning.

Since the linguistic evidence and the subject-matter are open to debate, it will be advantageous to examine Luke's narrative in some detail.

Verse 66

As often in introducing narratives,[3] Luke writes freely. His characteristic words appear in ὡς = 'when' (Luke nineteen, Acts twenty-nine), ἡμέρα used with γίνομαι (Luke three, Acts six), λαός, and τε. πρεσβυτέριον occurs here, Acts xxii. 5, and 1 Tim. iv. 14 only in the New Testament and συνέδριον here and thirteen or fourteen times in Acts. The only word which might suggest dependence on Mark is γραμματεῖς, which Luke often takes over from Mark, but uses very rarely in sections peculiar to himself (cf. xxiii. 10), preferring to use νομικός.[4] The parallel passage in Mark may be xv. 1, but Luke may be using this verse in xxiii. 1, and Easton thinks he would not have used it twice. As suggested above, the reference to the early morning suggests the use of a special tradition or source.

[1] *St Luke*, p. 276.   [2] *St Luke*, p. 339.
[3] Cf. Cadbury, *The Style and Literary Method of Luke*, pp. 105–15.
[4] Cf. G.D. Kilpatrick, *JTS*, NS, 1 (1950), 56–60.

Verses 67–8

Luke has no parallel to the Markan account of the false witnesses (Mk. xiv. 55–61), but begins with the challenge, 'If you are the Christ, tell us.' This corresponds to the question of Caiaphas in Mk. xiv. 61, 'Are you the Christ, the Son of the Blessed?', but it is less vivid and direct. In Mark Jesus replies explicitly 'I am', unless we read σὺ εἶπας ὅτι ἐγώ εἰμι.[1] In Luke a direct reply is avoided, 'If I tell you, you will not believe. If I ask you, you will not answer.' Some MSS add 'or release me',[2] a reading which Creed accepts on the ground that its omission may be explained by reluctance to make Jesus express or imply a wish to be released.[3] If the phrase is read, the distinctiveness of the Lukan reply is enhanced. ἐρωτάω is Lukan, but εἶπεν αὐτοῖς stands in Rehkopf's list. Easton thinks it is hopeless to derive 67*a* from Mark, and suggests that, while the saying is too indirect and obscure to be Luke's work, it 'corresponds entirely to the situation'.[4]

Verse 69

The use made of Ps. cx. 1 in Luke and Mark creates a difficult problem. Two independent sources might well refer to the same Old Testament passage, and in this case the parallel accounts would naturally share words and phrases in common. In the Septuagint, Ps. cx. 1 reads Εἶπεν ὁ κύριος τῷ κυρίῳ μου Κάθου ἐκ δεξιῶν μου. In their use of this passage Luke and Mark naturally use κάθημαι and ἐκ δεξιῶν, and ὁ υἱὸς τοῦ ἀνθρώπου is probably derived from Dan. vii. 13 (ὡς υἱὸς ἀνθρώπου). But why do they agree in using the participle καθήμενος and τῆς δυνάμεως? And why does Luke add τοῦ θεοῦ to δυνάμεως, which is a periphrasis for God? Is there not a case for presuming Luke's dependence on Mark? Modification of Mark is recognised as a possibility in *BTG*[5] but it is argued that the form of verse 69 is due to the drift of the Lukan narrative as a whole, especially as the question 'Are you then the Son of God?' is provoked, and immediately follows in verse 70. And there are other things to be said. Too much may be made of the common use of the participle.

---

[1] Cf. Taylor, *St Mark*, p. 568. It is read by Θ and other Caesarean MSS and by Origen.

[2] ἢ ἀπολύσητε.

[3] *St Luke*, p. 278.

[4] *St Luke*, p. 338.

[5] Pp. 50f.

It is a natural change in a semi-quotation,[1] and the use of the periphrastic future (ἔσται... καθήμενος) is not infrequent in Luke in non-Markan contexts.[2] It is less easy to explain the agreement in using τῆς δυνάμεως, for it is not present in Ps. cx. 1 and Dan. vii. 13, and the addition of τοῦ θεοῦ in Luke 'obscures the nature of the idiom'.[3] This addition may be an amplification of Mark ('the Power'), but it could have stood already in a non-Markan source, as it does in the parallel phrase τῶν ἀγγέλων τοῦ θεοῦ in the Lukan form of Q in Lk. xii. 8f. and in Lk. xv. 10.[4] Moreover, there is a striking difference in the application of the quotation. In Mark the priests are told that they will see the Son of Man sitting at the right hand of God; in Luke the fact of the *sessio ad dextram* is affirmed, and the quotation from Dan. vii. 13 (Mark καὶ ἐρχόμενον μετὰ τῶν νεφελῶν τοῦ οὐρανοῦ) is omitted. This difference may be a modification on the part of Luke, but against this suggestion is the fact that Dan. vii. 13 is quoted in Lk. xxi. 27. The omission therefore may be due to the use of a source. On the whole, the possibility that verse 69 is an editorial variant of Mk. xiv. 62 is not certain, although this explanation cannot be ruled out.

Verse 70

Luke shares ὁ υἱὸς τοῦ with Mk. xiv. 61 and ὁ δέ with 62, and has characteristic expressions in πάντες and πρός *c. acc.* after a verb of saying (ἔφη). He has ὑμεῖς λέγετε ὅτι ἐγώ εἰμι, 'It is you who say I am' (NEB), instead of Mark's strong affirmative 'I am', unless we read σὺ εἶπας... (see above on vv. 67–8). If we reject the latter reading the agreement with Mark is reduced, though not entirely removed. Of the verse as a whole Easton says, 'Again Lk is inexplicable as a revision of Mk.'[5]

Verse 71

In this verse Luke has τί ἔτι ἔχομεν μαρτυρίας χρείαν; and Mark τί ἔτι χρείαν ἔχομεν μαρτύρων; Both use ἀκούω, but Luke does

---

[1] Cf. Col. iii. 1, τὰ ἄνω ζητεῖτε, οὗ ὁ χριστός ἐστιν ἐν δεξιᾷ τοῦ θεοῦ καθήμενος.

[2] Cf. Lk. i. 20; v. 10; xii. 52; xvii. 35; xxi. 17; also the periphrastic imperative in xix. 17.

[3] Cf. G. Dalman, *The Words of Jesus*, p. 200.

[4] Cf. Dalman, *op. cit.* p. 197, 'In these cases τοῦ θεοῦ should clearly be erased, as it partially defeats the intention of the phrase.' I have treated the name 'the Power' in *The Names of Jesus*, p. 150.

[5] *St Luke*, p. 339.

6-2

not mention blasphemy and has ἀπὸ τοῦ στόματος αὐτοῦ, a noun which he has nine times in the Gospel and twelve times in Acts. Creed claims that dependence on Mark 'comes out clearly at v. 71'.[1] Streeter held the same view.[2]

Summary

The character of the narrative is very difficult to determine. It is difficult to believe that it is based solely on Mark or that it is entirely independent of Mark. Topical and linguistic features which point in one direction can be countered by evidence which favours the other. Apart from verse 66 there are few of Luke's characteristic words noted by Hawkins and still fewer listed by Rehkopf, and there is nothing common to Luke and John.[3] The difference in time and place in 66 strongly suggests the knowledge of a special tradition or source and to some degree this inference is supported, negatively by the absence of allusions to blasphemy and false witness, and positively by the different applications of Ps. cx. 1 in Luke and Mark and the evasive reply to the challenge of the priests in Luke. Easton's judgement sums up the situation best when he says that Luke's narrative cannot be understood as a revision of Mark 'although it doubtless contains reminiscences of Mk'.[4] Verse 71 is a near parallel to Mk. xiv. 63, but it lacks the clear-cut character of a Markan insertion comparable with those in Lk. xxiii. The opinion may be hazarded that, while Luke's special tradition knew of a morning trial, it contained no detailed account of the examination itself beyond the fact that it turned on the question of Messiahship.

14. THE TRIALS BEFORE PILATE AND HEROD

(Lk. xxiii. 1–25; cf. Mk. xv. 1–15;
Matt. xxvii. 1–2, 11–26)

[1] Καὶ ἀναστὰν ἅπαν τὸ πλῆθος αὐτῶν ἤγαγον αὐτὸν ἐπὶ τὸν Πειλᾶτον. [2] Ἤρξαντο δὲ κατηγορεῖν αὐτοῦ λέγοντες· τοῦτον εὕραμεν διαστρέφοντα τὸ ἔθνος ἡμῶν καὶ κωλύοντα φόρους

[1] *St Luke*, p. 278. [2] *FG*, p. 222.
[3] Cf. S. I. Buse, *NTS*, VII (1960), 71. [4] *St Luke*, p. 339.

Καίσαρι διδόναι καὶ λέγοντα ἑαυτὸν Χριστὸν βασιλέα εἶναι. [3] ὁ δὲ Πειλᾶτος ἠρώτησεν αὐτὸν λέγων· σὺ εἶ ὁ βασιλεὺς τῶν Ἰουδαίων; ὁ δὲ ἀποκριθεὶς αὐτῷ ἔφη· σὺ λέγεις. [4] ὁ δὲ Πειλᾶτος εἶπεν πρὸς τοὺς ἀρχιερεῖς καὶ τοὺς ὄχλους· οὐδὲν εὑρίσκω αἴτιον ἐν τῷ ἀνθρώπῳ τούτῳ. [5] οἱ δὲ ἐπίσχυον λέγοντες ὅτι ἀνασείει τὸν λαόν, διδάσκων καθ᾽ ὅλης τῆς Ἰουδαίας καὶ ἀρξάμενος ἀπὸ τῆς Γαλιλαίας ἕως ὧδε.

[6] Πειλᾶτος δὲ ἀκούσας ἐπηρώτησεν εἰ ὁ ἄνθρωπος Γαλιλαῖός ἐστιν, [7] καὶ ἐπιγνοὺς ὅτι ἐκ τῆς ἐξουσίας Ἡρώδου ἐστίν, ἀνέπεμψεν αὐτὸν πρὸς Ἡρώδην, ὄντα καὶ αὐτὸν ἐν Ἱεροσολύμοις ἐν ταύταις ταῖς ἡμέραις. [8] ὁ δὲ Ἡρώδης ἰδὼν τὸν Ἰησοῦν ἐχάρη λίαν· ἦν γὰρ ἐξ ἱκανῶν χρόνων θέλων ἰδεῖν αὐτὸν διὰ τὸ ἀκούειν περὶ αὐτοῦ, καὶ ἤλπιζέν τι σημεῖον ἰδεῖν ὑπ᾽ αὐτοῦ γινόμενον. [9] ἐπηρώτα δὲ αὐτὸν ἐν λόγοις ἱκανοῖς· αὐτὸς δὲ οὐδὲν ἀπεκρίνατο αὐτῷ. [10] εἱστήκεισαν δὲ οἱ ἀρχιερεῖς καὶ οἱ γραμματεῖς εὐτόνως κατηγοροῦντες αὐτοῦ. [11] ἐξουθενήσας δὲ αὐτὸν καὶ ὁ Ἡρώδης σὺν τοῖς στρατεύμασιν αὐτοῦ καὶ ἐμπαίξας, περιβαλὼν ἐσθῆτα λαμπρὰν ἀνέπεμψεν αὐτὸν τῷ Πειλάτῳ. [12] ἐγένοντο δὲ φίλοι ὅ τε Ἡρώδης καὶ ὁ Πειλᾶτος ἐν αὐτῇ τῇ ἡμέρᾳ μετ᾽ ἀλλήλων· προϋπῆρχον γὰρ ἐν ἔχθρᾳ ὄντες πρὸς αὐτούς.

[13] Πειλᾶτος δὲ συνκαλεσάμενος τοὺς ἀρχιερεῖς καὶ τοὺς ἄρχοντας καὶ τὸν λαὸν [14] εἶπεν πρὸς αὐτούς· προσηνέγκατέ μοι τὸν ἄνθρωπον τοῦτον ὡς ἀποστρέφοντα τὸν λαόν, καὶ ἰδοὺ ἐγὼ ἐνώπιον ὑμῶν ἀνακρίνας οὐθὲν εὗρον ἐν τῷ ἀνθρώπῳ τούτῳ αἴτιον ὧν κατηγορεῖτε κατ᾽ αὐτοῦ. [15] ἀλλ᾽ οὐδὲ Ἡρώδης· ἀνέπεμψεν γὰρ αὐτὸν πρὸς ἡμᾶς, καὶ ἰδοὺ οὐδὲν ἄξιον θανάτου ἐστὶν πεπραγμένον αὐτῷ. [16] παιδεύσας οὖν αὐτὸν ἀπολύσω. [18] Ἀνέκραγον δὲ πανπληθεὶ λέγοντες· αἶρε τοῦτον, ἀπόλυσον δὲ ἡμῖν τὸν Βαραββᾶν· [19] ὅστις ἦν διὰ στάσιν τινὰ γενομένην ἐν τῇ πόλει καὶ φόνον βληθεὶς ἐν τῇ φυλακῇ. [20] πάλιν δὲ ὁ Πειλᾶτος προσεφώνησεν αὐτοῖς, θέλων ἀπολῦσαι τὸν Ἰησοῦν. [21] οἱ δὲ ἐπεφώνουν λέγοντες· σταύρου σταύρου αὐτόν. [22] ὁ δὲ τρίτον εἶπεν πρὸς αὐτούς· τί γὰρ κακὸν ἐποίησεν οὗτος; οὐδὲν αἴτιον θανάτου εὗρον ἐν αὐτῷ· παιδεύσας οὖν αὐτὸν ἀπολύσω. [23] οἱ δὲ ἐπέκειντο φωναῖς μεγάλαις αἰτούμενοι αὐτὸν σταυρωθῆναι, καὶ

κατίσχυον αἱ φωναὶ αὐτῶν. [24] καὶ Πειλᾶτος ἐπέκρινεν γενέσθαι τὸ αἴτημα αὐτῶν· [25] ἀπέλυσεν δὲ τὸν διὰ στάσιν καὶ φόνον βεβλημένον εἰς φυλάκην, ὃν ᾐτοῦντο, τὸν δὲ Ἰησοῦν παρέδωκεν τῷ θελήματι αὐτῶν.

Note. Verse 17 is omitted by WH and Nestle (ἀνάγκην δὲ εἶχεν ἀπολύειν αὐτοῖς κατὰ ἑορτὴν ἕνα, ℵ W Δ Θ *et al.* minn. lat sy^p hl bo. Om. A B L Π 0124 *et al.* a fu sa bo. It is read after verse 19 by D sy^sc aeth.).

The numerical aspects of the narrative are as follows: of the 373 words of Lk. xxiii. 1–25 only fifty-two (or 13.9 per cent) are common to Mk. xv. 1–15, and if we omit from the comparison the Lukan account of the trial by Herod (verses 6–16), the percentage rises only to 27.2. Moreover, of the fifty-two words common to Luke and Mark, twenty-seven are accounted for by proper names, the verb 'to crucify', and instances of the use of δέ and the definite article. It is interesting to observe that no less than sixteen of the words in common occur in a single verse (Lk. xxiii. 3), a fact which raises the question whether this verse may not be a Markan addition. The narrative consists of three parts: (*a*) the examination by Pilate, (*b*) the examination before Herod, and (*c*) the rest of the trial by Pilate. As these sections differ in many ways it will be best to examine them separately.

(a) The examination by Pilate (xxiii. 1–5)

Apart from verse 3 there are only four words common to Luke and Mark and these mention Pilate twice. Almost certainly verse 3 is a Markan insertion in a non-Markan narrative. Luke's hand is seen in seven characteristic expressions, three in the first verse (ἀναστάς, ἅπαν τὸ πλῆθος, and ἄγω) and four in verses 2–5 (τούτον, ἐρωτάω, πρός, and λαός). Creed maintains that verse 3 is not an enrichment of Luke's narrative, since otherwise, when the priests have formulated their charges, Pilate replies forthwith, 'I find no fault in him.'[1] There is indeed a gap, and this is the reason for the insertion. In any case it only partially fills the gap, since of the three charges in verse 2 – political agitation, the forbidding of the payment of taxes, and royal claims – the insertion raises only the question of Messiahship, a

[1] *ET*, xlvi, 379.

charge to which Jesus agrees. This objection demands too much of the narrative and cannot stand against the fact that sixteen of the nineteen words in the verse are common to Mark. There is a Semitism in verse 5 in the phrase ἀρξάμενος ἀπό[1] which appears also in xxiv. 27, 47; Acts i. 22; Jn. viii. [9]**.

(b)   The examination before Herod (xxiii. 6–16)

This section is peculiar to Luke. It has nothing characteristic of Mark except οἱ γραμματεῖς in verse 10. Stanton observes that the account 'bears strong marks of having been indited by the evangelist himself'.[2] His distinctive words and phrases appear in ἐξουσία, ἐν ταύταις ταῖς ἡμέραις, χαίρω, ἱκανός (twice), χρόνοι, τι, σύν, τε, συνκαλέω, οἱ ἄρχοντες, λαός (twice), πρός c. acc., ἐνώπιον, and πράσσω. Further, ἀναπέμπω (Luke three times, Acts xxv. 21, Philem. 11**) and προϋπάρχω (here and Acts viii. 9**) are found almost entirely in Luke/Acts, verse 11 with its three participial clauses is 'skilfully balanced',[3] and the dative of the agent in 15 (αὐτῷ) is the one example of this construction in the New Testament.[4] Although οἱ γραμματεῖς is characteristic of Mark, we cannot claim that Luke of himself never uses it (cf. xxii. 66), and to excise 10–12 with sy[s] would be a doubtful expedient.[5] There is little to suggest the use of a source. Only two words from Rehkopf's list appear in the narrative (ἄξιος in 15 and χαίρειν in 8). Easton suggests derivation from L,[6] but this view is probable only if Luke is the author of that source[7] or if he has considerably rewritten the passage when composing the Gospel. Some knowledge of Johannine tradition is implied. The second of Pilate's three declarations of the innocence of Jesus, common to Luke and John, appears in verse 15, and the silence of Jesus is mentioned in verse 9 and Jn. xix. 9f.

---

[1] Cf. Moulton–Howard, *Grammar*, II, 454; Black, *Aramaic Approach to the Gospels and Acts*, p. 299.
[2] *GHD*, II, 307.
[3] *Ibid.*
[4] Cf. Moulton–Howard, *Grammar*, II, 459.
[5] Creed, *St Luke*, p. 282, observes that the verses are required to maintain the sequence of the narrative which has characteristic Lukan features.
[6] *St Luke*, p. 343.
[7] See pp. 125f. below for the conclusion that Luke is not the author of the special source.

(c) The examination by Pilate resumed (Lk. xxiii. 18–25)

The relation of the section to Mk. xv. 6–15 is difficult to determine. Verse 17 is generally rejected. It has points of contact with both Luke and John. Cf. ἀνάγκην ἔχειν in Lk. xiv. 18 and ἕνα in Jn. xviii. 39. But it shares κατὰ ἑορτήν with Mk. xv. 6. Without the verse the reference to Barabbas is introduced very abruptly. Whereas in Mk. xv. 8 the crowd assembles and asks Pilate to observe the custom of releasing a prisoner, in Luke, apart from 17, there is 'a general outcry'[1] at the proposal to release Jesus and a sudden demand for the release of Barabbas, 'Away with this man, and release to us Barabbas.' αἶρε recalls Jn. xix. 15, ἆρον ἆρον, σταύρωσον αὐτόν, but this comes later in John than the Barabbas story (Jn. xviii. 39f.). τοῦτον is Lukan and there are parallels to αἶρε in Acts xxi. 36, αἶρε αὐτόν, and xxii. 22. The sudden reference to Barabbas compels Luke to explain who he is, and although Luke and Mark have only two words in common, στάσις and φόνος, there is a broad resemblance between Lk. xxiii. 19 and Mk. xv. 7. It is not surprising that the Barabbas incident has been held to be a Markan insertion in Luke,[2] and that 20–2 have also been thought to be Markan.[3] τί γὰρ κακὸν ἐποίησεν in 22 agrees with Mk. xv. 14, except that in Luke κακόν precedes ἐποίησεν, and παιδεύσας οὖν αὐτὸν ἀπολύσω in 22b and 16 form a doublet. Can it be that in 23f. Luke returns to his special source? These suggestions cannot lightly be dismissed, but they are not conclusive. If the Barabbas incident is an insertion, we should expect the Markan text to be followed more closely. Of the twenty-six words in 18f., only six are common to Luke and Mark. We have seen that αἶρε is used similarly in Acts and that τοῦτον is Lukan. The same is true of τις in 19 and εἶπεν πρός c. acc. in 22. Further, προσφωνεῖν in 20 occurs six out of seven times in Luke/Acts, and ἐπιφωνεῖν in 21 and in the three other New Testament examples in Acts. Moreover, there is a further parallel with Johannine tradition in the third attempt of Pilate to release Jesus in 22. Luke's modification

---

[1] NEB.

[2] Cf. B. Weiss, Die Evangelien des Markus und Lukas (in Meyer's Commentary), p. 664; B. S. Easton, St Luke, p. 345.

[3] Easton cites Weiss for the view that the sudden divergence from Mark in 23 is doubtless due to a return to L.

of Mark or of his special source are equally possible, and the agreement of Luke with John makes the use of a non-Markan source the more probable alternative.

The agreements of 23f. with Mark are negligible. The two verbs ἐπίκειμαι[1] and κατισχύειν[2] have parallels elsewhere in Luke or Acts and ἐπικρίνειν is found here only in the New Testament. ὃν ᾐτοῦντο, 'whom they kept demanding',[3] is stressed and is probably intended to recall ὃν παρῃτοῦντο in Mk. xv. 6, and all the evangelists have παρέδωκεν, 'gave up'. The cadence of 25, and the emphasis on the enormity of the dreadful choice, together with the carefully constructed phrase τὸν διὰ στάσιν καὶ φόνον βεβλημένον εἰς φυλακήν, all point to composition by Luke, and it may be conjectured that he added the verse in the final stages of writing the Gospel.

Summary

The investigation shows that 1–5 is derived from a non-Markan source in which verse 3 has been inserted, and that 6–16 was composed by Luke himself out of tradition contained in the non-Markan source. The origin of 18–25 is more speculative. It appears to be derived from a non-Markan source to which verse 25 may have been added when the Third Gospel was composed.

15. THE JOURNEY TO THE CROSS

(Lk. xxiii. 26–32; cf. Mk. xv. 21; Matt. xxvii. 32)

[26] Καὶ ὡς ἀπήγαγον αὐτόν, ἐπιλαβόμενοι Σίμωνά τινα Κυρηναῖον ἐρχόμενον ἀπ' ἀγροῦ ἐπέθηκαν αὐτῷ τὸν σταυρὸν φέρειν ὄπισθεν τοῦ Ἰησοῦ. [27] ἠκολούθει δὲ αὐτῷ πολὺ πλῆθος τοῦ λαοῦ καὶ γυναικῶν, αἳ ἐκόπτοντο καὶ ἐθρήνουν αὐτόν. [28] στραφεὶς δὲ πρὸς αὐτὰς Ἰησοῦς εἶπεν· θυγατέρες Ἰερουσαλήμ, μὴ κλαίετε ἐπ' ἐμέ· πλὴν ἐφ' ἑαυτὰς κλαίετε καὶ ἐπὶ τὰ τέκνα ὑμῶν. [29] ὅτι ἰδοὺ ἔρχονται ἡμέραι ἐν αἷς ἐροῦσιν· μακάριαι αἱ στεῖραι, καὶ αἱ κοιλίαι αἳ οὐκ ἐγέννησαν, καὶ μαστοὶ οἳ οὐκ ἔθρεψαν. [30] τότε ἄρξονται λέγειν τοῖς ὄρεσιν· πέσατε ἐφ' ἡμᾶς, καὶ τοῖς

[1] Lk. v. 1; xxiii. 23; Acts xxvii. 20; Jn. xi. 38; xxi. 9; 1 Cor. ix. 16; Heb. ix. 10**.
[2] Lk. xxi. 36; xxiii. 23; Matt. xvi. 18**.
[3] Cf. A. Plummer, *St Luke*, p. 527.

THE PASSION NARRATIVE OF ST LUKE

βουνοῖς· καλύψατε ἡμᾶς· [31] ὅτι εἰ ἐν τῷ ὑγρῷ ξύλῳ ταῦτα ποιοῦσιν, ἐν τῷ ξηρῷ τί γένηται; [32] ἤγοντο δὲ καὶ ἕτεροι δύο κακοῦργοι σὺν αὐτῷ ἀναιρεθῆναι.

This is a case in which the numerical argument alone is conclusive. Of 110 words Luke shares only fourteen with Mark. Verse 26, which contains eleven Markan words out of nineteen, is clearly derived from Mk. xv. 20b–21, as the common use of Σίμωνά... Κυρηναῖον ἐρχόμενον ἀπ' ἀγροῦ shows. Linguistic arguments confirm this view. The rare word ἀγγαρεύουσιν is dropped and ἀπήγαγον is suggested by ἐξάγουσιν in Mk. xv. 20b. ὡς, ἐπιλαμβάνομαι, and τις are Lukan, and the statement that Simon carried the cross after Jesus is a correction of the tradition in Jn. xix. 17, that Jesus carried his own cross.

Verses 27–31 are peculiar to Luke. Verse 32 shares three words with Mk. xv. 27 (δύο, σὺν αὐτῷ), but the difference of position and the presence of five expressions characteristic of Luke (ἄγω, δὲ καί, ἕτερος, σύν, ἀναιρεῖν) suggests that, like 27–31, it is non-Markan. In addition to these words, 27f. include five more (πλῆθος, λαός, στραφείς, κλαίω (twice), and πλήν), but the last three are listed by Rehkopf. στεῖρος is found mainly in Luke (i. 7, 36; xxiii. 29; Gal. iv. 27**) and κακοῦργος appears three times (xxiii. 32, 33, 39) and in 2 Tim. ii. 9**. This linguistic evidence might seem to point to the conclusion that the narrative of the women of Jerusalem was freely composed by Luke himself. This would be a hasty deduction, for there are indications of the use of an earlier source. Rehkopf lists καὶ ὡς (temporal), the vocative θυγατέρες Ἰερουσαλήμ, ἐρεῖν, ἄρξομαι c. infin., στραφείς, κλαίειν (twice), and πλήν as illustrative of pre-Lukan usage. ἰδού has a Semitic flavour and the impersonal plural ποιοῦσιν is probably an Aramaism.[1] These expressions outnumber Luke's characteristic words and support the view that Luke is editing a non-Markan source.[2]

We conclude that verse 26 is a Markan addition prefixed to a non-Markan narrative.

[1] Cf. Black, *Aramaic Approach to the Gospels and Acts*, pp. 126f.
[2] In view of Jeremias's discussion of the crucifixion narrative which follows, it should be noted that he includes xxiii. 26–32 with it.

16. THE CRUCIFIXION

(Lk. xxiii. 33–49; cf. Mk. xv. 22–41;
Matt. xxvii. 33–56)

[33] Καὶ ὅτε ἦλθον ἐπὶ τὸν τόπον τὸν καλούμενον Κρανίον, ἐκεῖ ἐσταύρωσαν αὐτὸν καὶ τοὺς κακούργους, ὃν μὲν ἐκ δεξιῶν, ὃν δὲ ἐξ ἀριστερῶν. [34] ὁ δὲ Ἰησοῦς ἔλεγεν· πάτερ ἄφες αὐτοῖς· οὐ γὰρ οἴδασιν τί ποιοῦσιν. διαμεριζόμενοι δὲ τὰ ἱμάτια αὐτοῦ ἔβαλον κλήρους. [35] καὶ εἱστήκει ὁ λαὸς θεωρῶν. ἐξεμυκτήριζον δὲ καὶ οἱ ἄρχοντες λέγοντες· ἄλλους ἔσωσεν, σωσάτω ἑαυτόν, εἰ οὗτός ἐστιν ὁ Χριστὸς τοῦ Θεοῦ ὁ ἐκλεκτός. [36] ἐνέπαιξαν δὲ αὐτῷ καὶ οἱ στρατιῶται προσερχόμενοι, ὄξος προσφέροντες αὐτῷ [37] καὶ λέγοντες· εἰ σὺ εἶ ὁ βασιλεὺς τῶν Ἰουδαίων, σῶσον σεαυτόν. [38] ἦν δὲ καὶ ἐπιγραφὴ ἐπ᾽ αὐτῷ· ὁ βασιλεὺς τῶν Ἰουδαίων οὗτος.

[39] Εἷς δὲ τῶν κρεμασθέντων κακούργων ἐβλασφήμει αὐτόν· οὐχὶ σὺ εἶ ὁ Χριστός; σῶσον σεαυτὸν καὶ ἡμᾶς. [40] ἀποκριθεὶς δὲ ὁ ἕτερος ἐπιτιμῶν αὐτῷ ἔφη· οὐδὲ φοβῇ σὺ τὸν θεόν, ὅτι ἐν τῷ αὐτῷ κρίματι εἶ; [41] καὶ ἡμεῖς μὲν δικαίως, ἄξια γὰρ ὧν ἐπράξαμεν ἀπολαμβάνομεν, οὗτος δὲ οὐδὲν ἄτοπον ἔπραξεν. [42] καὶ ἔλεγεν· Ἰησοῦ, μνήσθητί μου ὅταν ἔλθῃς εἰς τὴν βασιλείαν σου. [43] καὶ εἶπεν αὐτῷ· ἀμήν σοι λέγω, σήμερον μετ᾽ ἐμοῦ ἔσῃ ἐν τῷ παραδείσῳ. [44] Καὶ ἦν ἤδη ὡσεὶ ὥρα ἕκτη καὶ σκότος ἐγένετο ἐφ᾽ ὅλην τὴν γῆν ἕως ὥρας ἐνάτης [45] τοῦ ἡλίου ἐκλιπόντος· ἐσχίσθη δὲ τὸ καταπέτασμα τοῦ ναοῦ μέσον. [46] καὶ φωνήσας φωνῇ μεγάλῃ ὁ Ἰησοῦς εἶπεν· πάτερ, εἰς χεῖράς σου παρατίθεμαι τὸ πνεῦμά μου. τοῦτο δὲ εἰπὼν ἐξέπνευσεν. [47] ἰδὼν δὲ ὁ ἑκατοντάρχης τὸ γενόμενον ἐδόξαζεν τὸν θεὸν λέγων· ὄντως ὁ ἄνθρωπος οὗτος δίκαιος ἦν. [48] καὶ πάντες οἱ συμπαραγενόμενοι ὄχλοι ἐπὶ τὴν θεωρίαν ταύτην, θεωρήσαντες τὰ γενόμενα, τύπτοντες τὰ στήθη, ὑπέστρεφον. [49] Εἱστήκεισαν δὲ πάντες οἱ γνωστοὶ αὐτῷ ἀπὸ μακρόθεν, καὶ γυναῖκες αἱ συνακολουθοῦσαι αὐτῷ ἀπὸ τῆς Γαλιλαίας, ὁρῶσαι ταῦτα.

Of the 265 words in the narrative only seventy-four (or 28.3 per cent) are common to Luke and Mark, and of these nearly a quarter occur in two successive verses (44f.). This low percentage is due partly to the fact that several details in Mark have no parallel in Luke, while Luke has a number of features peculiar to itself.

The Markan details with no parallel in Luke include the following:

(1) The name 'Golgotha'.

(2) The statement that wine was rejected by Jesus.

(3) The reference to the time of the crucifixion ('the third hour').

(4) The reference to the railing of those who passed by, wagging their heads and saying, 'Ha! thou that destroyest the temple, and buildest it in three days, save thyself, and come down from the cross.'

(5) Some of the words of the chief priests (Luke, 'the rulers'): 'Let the Christ, the King of Israel, now come down from the cross, that we may see and believe.'

(6) The statement that those who were crucified with him (i.e. both) reproached him.

(7) The cry, 'Eloi, Eloi, lama sabachthani.'

(8) The statement that the bystanders supposed that Jesus called for Elijah: 'Let be; let us see whether Elijah cometh to take him down.'

Features peculiar to Luke are:

(1) The word 'malefactors'.

(2) The prayer, 'Father, forgive them; for they know not what they do.'

(3) The words, 'And the people stood beholding.'

(4) The phrase 'his chosen'.

(5) The statement that the soldiers mocked Jesus, offering Him vinegar.

(6) The story of the penitent robber and the words of his companion, 'Art not thou the Christ? save thyself and us.'

(7) The recording together of the miraculous darkness and the rending of the temple veil.

(8) The phrase 'the sun's light failing'.

(9) The words of the centurion, 'Certainly this was a righteous man.'

The small number of words in common with Mark and the differences between Luke and Mark in subject-matter suggest that Luke's source is non-Markan. This suggestion is considerably strengthened when the uneven *distribution* of the words in common with Mark is studied, for in several cases these are found in passages which appear to be Markan insertions.

Possible Markan insertions in Lk. xxiii. 33–49

(1) *Lk. xxiii. 34b*

'And parting his garments among them, they cast lots.' This passage is a quotation from Ps. xxii. 8 and might appear independently in the two narratives. But of the seven Greek words six agree with Mk. xv. 24*b* and the quotation comes in abruptly in Luke. It may therefore be a Markan insertion.

(2) *Lk. xxiii. 38*

'And there was also a superscription over him, This is the King of the Jews.' The common words number six out of eleven. Further, the verse is loosely connected in its Lukan context. It does not stand at the beginning as in Mk. xv. 26, but slips in as a kind of afterthought suggested by the soldiers' taunt, 'If you are the King of the Jews, save yourself.' Moreover, as we shall see later, the verse interrupts a deliberately constructed sequence in Luke's narrative. This fact, together with its topical connexion with 37, and its linguistic agreement with Mk. xv. 26, leads us to suspect that it is probably a Markan insertion.

(3) *Lk. xxiii. 44f.*

'And it was now about the sixth hour, and a darkness came over the whole land until the ninth hour, the sun's light failing: and the veil of the temple was rent in twain.' If any hesitation is felt about the two preceding passages, none can arise in the case of the present passage. Here out of twenty-six Greek words no less than seventeen are common to Luke and Mark. Nor is this all: in Mark the darkness and the rending are mentioned in different parts of the story, the rending following the reference to the death of Jesus. In Luke, on the contrary, the two incidents have been brought together, and both immediately precede the dying cry of Jesus. We can only suppose that these incidents have been taken from Mark and conjoined by the evangelist. But, if so, we must look upon the passage as an insertion in Luke; for it is impossible to suppose that the two have first been connected and then made the pivot around which a new rendering in the Lukan story turns. Moreover, if we omit the passage, the Lukan narrative does not suffer; it actually gains in dramatic force. For, with the omission, the promise to the penitent robber, 'Today you will be with me in Paradise', is immediately followed by the death-cry, 'And crying with a loud voice, Jesus said, "Father, into thy hands I commend my spirit": and having said this he expired.'

(4) *Lk. xxiii. 49*

'And all his friends stood at a distance, and women who had accompanied him from Galilee, and saw these things.' This passage also may be a Markan addition. Of its eighteen words nine are common to Luke and Mark, and it stands just where the Markan passage stands, at the end of the narrative. It lacks the names of the women as given by Mark, and leads on to the account of the burial and the subsequent action of the women in 50–6, forming a kind of doublet with 55. Possibly the verse is dependent on Ps. xxxviii. 11, καὶ οἱ ἔγγιστά μου μακρόθεν ἔστησαν, and Ps. lxxxviii. 8, ἐμάκρυνας τοὺς γνωστούς μου ἀπ' ἐμοῦ,[1] but the agreement with Mk. xv. 40f. in vocabulary, context, and literary purpose suggests that the basic source is Mark.

The linguistic features in the narrative

These will be studied best if we examine separately the three sections, Lk. xxiii. 33–8, 39–43, and 44–9.

(1) *Lk. xxiii. 33–8 (the crucifixion)*

In the two Markan insertions (34*b* and 38) only one expression, δὲ καί, is characteristic of Luke. Both διαμερίζω and κλῆρος are freely used in Luke/Acts, but both are taken over from Mark. No word in these two passages is listed by Rehkopf.

In contrast, there are 'Lukan' words in the rest of 33–8, καλούμενος, λαός, ἄρχοντες, and δὲ καί (twice), and other words which are significant for the question of authorship. See κακοῦργος, μὲν...δέ, διαμερίζω (Luke/Acts 8/11), κλῆρος (Luke/Acts 6/11), ἕστηκα (cf. xxiii. 10, 49), ἐκμυκτηρίζω (Lk. xvi. 14**), ὁ ἐκλεκτός (cf. Lk. ix. 35), ἐμπαίζω (cf. Lk. xxii. 63), στρατιώτης (Lk. vii. 8, Acts (13)), βασιλεύς (of Christ) (cf. Lk. xix. 38; xxiii. 2f., 38). There are no words from the section in Rehkopf's list. These facts reveal the considerable extent of Luke's diction, but whether he is recording oral tradition or embellishing a non-Markan source is not clear. As we shall see, the record in

---

[1] Cf. Creed, *St Luke*, p. 288.

Lk. xxiii. 44–9 and the structure of the section (see below) suggest the adaptation of an earlier source.

(2) *Lk. xxiii. 39–43 (the penitent robber)*

This section is peculiar to Luke. In it there are many signs of Luke's hand. The following 'Lukan' words occur: ἕτερος, πράσσω (twice), ἀπολαμβάνω, μιμνήσκομαι, and ὅς in attraction. See also κρεμάννυμι (Luke (1), Acts (3), Matt. (2), and Gal. iii. 13**), κακοῦργος (cf. v. 32), βλασφημέω (cf. v. 65), ἀποκριθεὶς... ἔφη, κρίμα in a forensic sense (cf. Lk. xxiv. 20), μὲν... δέ (cf. Lk. xxiii. 33, 56), ἄτοπος (cf. Acts xxv. 5; xxviii. 6; 2 Thess. iii. 2**). Again, as in vv. 33–8, it is clear that Luke has contributed very much to the composition of the narrative. Stanton[1] includes it in the nine sections in which the literary form 'should in all probability be attributed to the author himself'. It may be, however, that this opinion needs reconsideration, for Rehkopf lists features which point to pre-Lukan speech-usage. These include φοβέομαι (of fearing God), ἄξιος, μιμνήσκομαι, the vocative Ἰησοῦ, ἀπολαμβάνω, and εἶπεν αὐτῷ. It will be seen that ἀπολαμβάνω and μιμνήσκομαι occur in both lists, but in view of their distribution in Luke, Rehkopf has the better claim upon them. If so, the presumption is that Luke is editing a pre-Lukan source.

(3) *Lk. xxiii. 44–9 (the death of Jesus)*

'Lukan' words occur both in the insertions in 44f. and 49 (ὡσεί, γίνομαι ἐπί, γνωστοί used with πάντες) and in the rest of the section (δοξάζειν τὸν θεόν, and ὑποστρέφειν). Note also μέσος (cf. Acts i. 18), the σύν compound in συμπαραγίνομαι,[2] φωνήσας φωνῇ (cf. i. 42; ix. 14; Acts v. 28; xvi. 28; xxviii. 10), ἑκατοντάρχης (Lk. vii. 2, 6; Acts (13)), τὸ γενόμενον (cf. Lk. viii. 34; xxiv. 12; Acts iv. 21; v. 7; xiii. 12), ὄντως (xxiv. 34*), τὰ γενόμενα (cf. the sing. above), εἱστήκεισαν δέ (cf. xxiii. 10, 35). The words from Rehkopf's list are few and are limited to the Markan insertions (ἤδη, ἐκλείπειν, μακρόθεν). It does not necessarily follow that the section is freely composed by Luke

---

[1] *GHD*, II, 308–10.

[2] Fifty-two words, chiefly verbs, compounded with σύν, occur only, or most frequently, in Luke/Acts, and sixty-three in the Pauline epistles. Cf. Stanton, *GHD*, II, 290.

without the use of a source. As in the case of Lk. xxiii. 33–8, the structure (see below) may account for the absence of a pre-Lukan vocabulary. Moreover, the stylistic phenomena suggest a Lukan embellishment of sources, Mark and a special source. Signs pointing in this direction are the genitive absolute, τοῦ ἡλίου ἐκλιπόντος, the use of μέσος, and the many participles both adjectival and adverbial (ten in number). Cf. συμπαραγινό-μενοι used attributively in v. 48, a construction of which Luke is fond (cf. i. 1; xx. 1; xxii. 52). Further, it is very improbable that δίκαιος in the centurion's confession (v. 47) is a modification of υἱὸς θεοῦ in Mk. xv. 39. A problem is presented by ἐξέπνευσεν, 'expired', in v. 46, the only word common to Mk. xv. 37 (cf. xv. 39) and found in these passages alone in the New Testament. No completely satisfactory explanation can be given, but Easton suggests that the Markan word is used to replace some less dignified word in the source.[1] Alternatively, it is possible that the verb was taken over from Mark in the last stages of the composition of the Third Gospel. Apart from this difficulty the section, like vv. 33–8, appears to be derived from a pre-Lukan source. The entire narrative, 33–49, it may be suggested, is the Lukan re-setting of an earlier source supplemented by Markan additions in vv. 34b, 38, 44f., and 49. The bearing of the structure of 33–49 upon these possibilities must now be considered.

The structure of the Lukan narrative

Apart from the passages which appear to be Markan additions it is significant that a deliberately constructed sequence is visible in the rest of Luke's narrative.[2] Luke appears to have been deeply impressed by the contrast between the figure of Jesus and all the actors in the crucifixion story. He names the different classes and types of persons present one by one and gives their words and comments. The picture begins at verse 35 where with a few strokes of the pen he describes a large silent crowd in the words, 'And the people stood beholding.' It is noticeable that here and throughout the people are silent, until at the end we see them returning to Jerusalem, smiting their breasts. Stunned and bewildered, they present a sharp contrast to the rulers, the soldiers, and the malefactors, whose words in turn the evangelist records. First, we have a reference to the rulers and what they

---

[1] St Luke, p. 352.   [2] Cf. BTG, pp. 57–9.

say (v. 35*b*), then to the soldiers and their taunt (vv. 36f.), then to the malefactors and their words (vv. 39ff.). All call upon Jesus to save himself, but the rulers address him as God's Elect One, the soldiers as the King of the Jews, both in mockery. The penitent robber confesses Jesus' innocence and asks to be remembered when Jesus comes to his kingdom, and the centurion bears witness also to his innocence. Into this well-conceived narrative, surely a product of conscious art, the Markan insertions break clumsily, impairing the unity and dramatic force of the story, while v. 49, if it is a Markan addition, looks forward to the action of the women.

The original Lukan narrative

It will be useful to supply the original Lukan narrative in order to estimate the significance of structure. Omitting the Markan insertions the narrative is as follows:

And when they came to the place called The Skull, there they crucified him and the criminals one on the right and the other on the left. And Jesus said, 'Father, forgive them; for they know not what they are doing.' And the people stood looking on. And the rulers mocked him saying, 'He saved others; let him save himself, if he is God's anointed, his Chosen One.' The soldiers also mocked him, approaching him and offering him sour wine and saying, 'If you are the King of the Jews, save yourself.' And one of the criminals who hung with him railed at him, 'Are you not the Messiah? Save yourself and us.' But the other answered rebuking him, 'Do you not even fear God, seeing you are under the same condemnation? And we indeed justly, for we have received the due recompense for what we have done. But this man has done nothing wrong.' And he said, 'Jesus, remember me when you come into your kingdom.' And he said to him, 'Truly I say to you, today you will be with me in Paradise.' And crying with a loud voice Jesus said, 'Father, into thy hands I commend my spirit.' And having said this he expired. And the centurion seeing what had happened glorified God saying, 'Certainly this man was innocent.' And all the crowds which had come together to see the sight, having beheld what had happened beat their breasts and returned.

In the Greek of the above passage some of the words are common to Mark and Luke,[1] but they belong to the substance of the story and without them it could not be told. The only significant word in common is ἐξέπνευσεν, which has been mentioned earlier.[2]

Jeremias has discussed the structure of Luke's narrative of the

---

[1] See p. 91.   [2] See p. 96.

crucifixion from another point of view and comes to the conclusion that it is based on a non-Markan source.[1] He supports this
claim by numbering fourteen separate details in Mark's account
and seventeen in Luke, and by setting against the Lukan series the
corresponding numbers of the Markan series. Thus numbered the
series of Markan details in Luke is 1, 6, 2, 6, 4, 8, 10, 7, 5, 9, 12,
11, 13, 14. From this arrangement he is clearly justified in maintaining that, if Mark had been Luke's source, Luke's narrative
would be 'completely muddled up' (*vollständig durcheinandergewirbelt*). This would be entirely contrary to Luke's manner of
using Mark, and it is reasonable to conclude that in his narrative
Luke is following his special source.

Jeremias does not mention the passages I have discussed as
possible Markan insertions, but it is a confirmation of his hypothesis that these stand in Luke in the same order in which they
appear in Mark. This fact will be seen in the following table:

$$
\begin{array}{l}
\text{Lk. xxiii. 26} = \text{Mk. xv. 20}b\text{–21} \\
\text{Lk. xxiii. 34}b = \text{Mk. xv. 24}b \\
\text{Lk. xxiii. 38} = \text{Mk. xv. 26} \\
\text{Lk. xxiii. 44f.} = \text{Mk. xv. 33, 38} \\
\text{Lk. xxiii. 49} = \text{Mk. xv. 40f.}
\end{array}
$$

Expressed in the numbers assigned to the Markan series by
Jeremias, the common details are nos. 1, 4, 5, 9, 12, 14. Of these,
nos. 1 and 14 cannot well be otherwise than the first and last
details in the crucifixion narrative, but the rest owe their position
to the evangelist who inserts them. They are found in Luke in the
order in which they appear in Mark. It is remarkable that, in a
narrative which can be described as 'completely muddled up' if
Luke's basic source is Mark, this agreement in the order of
features common to Mark and Luke should be exact. The presumption is that Luke's account of the crucifixion is based on his
special source (L, or, as it is sometimes designated, S), supplemented by extracts from Mark. Apparently, reading his special
source in the light of Mk. xv. 22–41, he notes interesting and
important details which he desires to add to his original account.[2]

[1] *NTS*, IV (Jan. 1958), 115–19.
[2] Cited from my article, 'The Narrative of the Crucifixion', *NTS*, VIII
(July 1962), 333f.

Summary

In view of the arguments summarised above, statistical, linguistic, and structural, we conclude that in Lk. xxiii. 33–49 verses 34*b*, 38, 44f., and 49 are Markan insertions or additions in a non-Markan source.

17. THE BURIAL

(Lk. xxiii. 50–4; cf. Mk. xv. 42–7;
Matt. xxvii. 57–61)

[50] Καὶ ἰδοὺ ἀνὴρ ὀνόματι Ἰωσὴφ βουλευτὴς ὑπάρχων, ἀνὴρ ἀγαθὸς καὶ δίκαιος, — [51] οὗτος οὐκ ἦν συνκατατεθειμένος τῇ βουλῇ καὶ τῇ πράξει αὐτῶν, — ἀπὸ Ἀριμαθαίας πόλεως τῶν Ἰουδαίων, ὃς προσεδέχετο τὴν βασιλείαν τοῦ θεοῦ, [52] οὗτος προσελθὼν τῷ Πειλάτῳ ᾐτήσατο τὸ σῶμα τοῦ Ἰησοῦ, [53] καὶ καθελὼν ἐνετύλιξεν αὐτὸ σινδόνι, καὶ ἔθηκεν αὐτὸν ἐν μνήματι λαξευτῷ, οὗ οὐκ ἦν οὐδεὶς οὔπω κείμενος. [54] καὶ ἡμέρα ἦν Παρασκευῆς, καὶ σάββατον ἐπέφωσκεν.

Like the account of Peter's denial the story of Joseph of Arimathaea and of the burial of Jesus is derived from Mark. The percentage of words in common is 44.6. This percentage does not fully disclose the extent of dependence, for Luke has polished the style of his source and added a number of explanatory comments. Lk. xxiii. 50–4 is Mark's story abbreviated and expanded. Thus, it is explained that Joseph, although a βουλευτής, had not consented to the counsel and deed of the priests. Arimathaea is designated 'a city of the Jews', and the tomb is described as 'hewn in stone, where never man had yet lain' (cf. Jn. xix. 41). Further, the Lukan context contains phenomena which appear to be modifications due to the insertion of the burial story. For in xxiii. 49 and xxiii. 55 there is a doublet which owes its existence to the separation of passages originally conjoined. In verse 49 we read of 'women who had accompanied him from Galilee' and in 55 of 'the women who had come with him from Galilee'. The former passage has no article with γυναῖκες. Hence it is that in the second passage αἱ γυναῖκες is resumptive, and a second reference to Galilee has been added in consequence of the insertion of the burial story. The non-Markan character of 55f. has yet to be discussed, but apart from this the evidence suggests that the account of the burial has been taken from Mark. The change of the position of the temporal statement in 54, 'And it was the day of the Preparation', from the beginning of the story (as in Mark) to the end, is probably due to the account of the action of the women which follows. This point will be considered later.

Points in the Markan narrative which have no parallel in Luke appear to be omitted for editorial reasons. Thus Luke does not record that it 'took courage' on the part of Joseph to make his request for the body of Jesus and that Pilate inquired from the centurion whether he was already dead. He does not mention the buying of the linen shroud and the rolling of a stone against the door of the tomb. These omissions are due to the desire for abbreviation.

The linguistic facts confirm the view that Mark is Luke's source. Luke often edits the introductions to new sections with the greatest independence.[1] It is not surprising, therefore, that in verses 50 and 51 several characteristic Lukan words appear (ἀνήρ, ὀνόματι, ὑπάρχω, βουλή). With ἀνὴρ ἀγαθός cf. Acts xi. 24. The periphrastic perfect is used in 51 as elsewhere, and πόλις followed by a proper name is characteristic. προσδέχομαι is also a Lukan word, but here it is taken over from Mark. The substitution of ἐνετύλιξεν for ἐνείλησεν is probably intentional, since ἐνειλέω is often, though not always, used in a bad sense.[2] λαξευτός, found here only in the New Testament, may have been chosen as an abbreviation of Mark's ὃ ἦν λελατομημένον ἐκ πέτρας. οὗ = 'where' is Lukan.

There is little to suggest that Luke is dependent on any written source other than Mark. Easton[3] thinks that the cumbrous character of 50f. is due to the fusing of L and Mark, and further that Luke 'cannot be credited with λαξευτός', but, as we have seen, the linguistic facts can be explained otherwise. No words or phrases from Rehkopf's list appear in the narrative, with the exception of κεῖμαι (also in Hawkins's list), and the only

---

[1] Cf. Cadbury, *The Style and Literary Method of Luke*, p. 105; Rehkopf, *LS*, pp. 10, 34f.
[2] Cf. Taylor, *St Mark*, p. 601.
[3] *St Luke*, p. 355.

un-Lukan expression is ἰδού used without a verb. The statement that the tomb was one in which no man had lain may reflect a knowledge of Johannine tradition,[1] but it hardly requires the use of a written source.

Summary

The investigation has shown that in the account of the burial Luke's source is Mark, without any clear sign of a second source except a knowledge of Johannine tradition. This hypothesis does not mean that Luke had no knowledge of the burial from other sources. The primitive summary of the *kerygma* in 1 Cor. xv. 3–7 includes the statement, 'For I delivered to you as of first importance what I received ... that he was buried', and Luke agrees with John in saying that the tomb was one in which 'no one had yet been laid'. Lk. xxiii. 50–4 may have replaced a brief reference to the burial, but of this we have no evidence. Alternatively, the Passion narrative may have ended with the centurion's confession. This conclusion, however, depends on the view we take of the action of the women described in Lk. xxiii. 55f. and the resurrection narratives of Lk. xxiv, and these questions remain to be considered.

18. THE ACTION OF THE WOMEN

(Lk. xxiii. 55–6a; cf. Mk. xv. 47 – xvi. 1;
Matt. xxvii. 61; xxviii. 1)

Lk. xxiii. 55–6a

[55] Κατακολουθήσασαι δὲ αἱ γυναῖκες, αἵτινες ἦσαν συνεληλυ-θυῖαι ἐκ τῆς Γαλιλαίας αὐτῷ, ἐθεάσαντο τὸ μνημεῖον καὶ ὡς ἐτέθη τὸ σῶμα αὐτοῦ, [56a] ὑποστρέψασαι δὲ ἡτοίμασαν ἀρώματα καὶ μύρα.

Mk. xv. 47 – xvi. 1

[47] ἡ δὲ Μαρία ἡ Μαγδαληνὴ καὶ Μαρία ἡ Ἰωσῆτος ἐθεώρουν ποῦ τέθειται [xvi. 1] καὶ διαγενομένου τοῦ σαββάτου Μαρία ἡ Μαγδα-ληνὴ καὶ Μαρία ἡ τοῦ Ἰακώβου καὶ Σαλώμη ἠγόρασαν ἀρώματα ἵνα ἐλθοῦσαι ἀλείψωσιν αὐτόν.

[1] Cf. Jn. xix. 41, ἐν ᾧ οὐδέπω οὐδεὶς ἦν τεθειμένος.

It will be seen that the two passages have little in common. Only three of the twenty-six words of the passage in Luke are common to Mark, and there is no parallel to the names in Mark. There is a resemblance between ἐθεάσαντο...ὡς ἐτέθη τὸ σῶμα αὐτοῦ (Lk. xxiii. 55) and ἐθεώρουν ποῦ τέθειται (Mk. xv. 47) which may be thought to imply dependence, but it is not close. Further, the reference to the tomb comes in somewhat abruptly, if the burial story is a Markan addition.

The statement of 56*a* about the preparation of spices and ointments stands in complete contrast to Mk. xvi. 1, for according to Mark it is *after the Sabbath is past* that the women buy the spices. This assertion is consistent with the Markan story. According to Mark's account there is no time for the purchase and preparation of the spices before the Sabbath. In fact, there is barely time for the burial itself, for even before Joseph has interviewed Pilate the beginning of the Sabbath is very near (cf. Mk. xv. 42). It is still the Preparation (i.e. Friday), but 'even was now come', and with sunset the Sabbath begins. Clearly everything is done with the greatest possible haste.

With such a source before him it is difficult to think that Luke would have spoken of the return of the women and the preparation of spices *before* the Sabbath, for he says explicitly, 'And on the sabbath they rested according to the commandment' (56*b*). It is only a partial answer to say that Luke has extended the interval by transferring the temporal statement of Mk. xv. 42 to the end of his account of the burial, so that it now refers to the subsequent action of the women. It is more satisfactory to think that he is following a different tradition, which required a change in the temporal statement in consequence of his insertion of the burial story in his existing and independent non-Markan narrative.[1]

Returning to verse 55 we may say that if 56*a* is non-Markan, the same must be true of the two verses, for they are closely connected. If the reference to the tomb is thought to be too abrupt, we may reasonably ask if the verse has been modified in consequence of the insertion of the burial story. Has that narrative replaced a simple reference to burial? A different tradition

[1] Kirsopp Lake's suggestion in *The Historical Evidence for the Resurrection of Jesus Christ*, p. 59, that Luke had forgotten the Jewish time-reckoning, does not seem satisfactory. See *BTG*, pp. 61f.

appears to be suggested when Luke, in agreement with Jn. xix. 41, speaks of 'a tomb that was hewn in stone, where never man had yet lain', although John simply describes the tomb as 'new'. Apparently Luke used a source which, after a passing reference to the burial, told how the women beheld the tomb, and then, returning to Jerusalem, prepared spices and ointments before the Sabbath began.

So far as they go, linguistic considerations support the view that the passage is non-Markan; it consists of a well-constructed sentence, in which participles are skilfully used. Even in so short a passage a σύν compound and a 'Lukan' word (ὑποστρέφω) appear, but there are no words or phrases from Rehkopf's list. The presumption is that Luke himself rewrote the account given in his special source, to serve as an introduction to the narrative of the visit to the tomb.

Summary

On all counts Lk. xxiii. 55–6a is non-Markan.

19. THE VISIT OF THE WOMEN TO THE TOMB

(Lk. xxiii. 56b – xxiv. 11; cf. Mk. xvi. 1–8;
Matt. xxviii. 1–8)

[xxiii. 56b] Καὶ τὸ μὲν σάββατον ἡσύχασαν κατὰ τὴν ἐντολήν [xxiv. 1] τῇ δὲ μιᾷ τῶν σαββάτων ὄρθρου βαθέως ἐπὶ τὸ μνῆμα ἦλθον φέρουσαι ἃ ἡτοίμασαν ἀρώματα. [2] εὗρον δὲ τὸν λίθον ἀποκεκυλισμένον ἀπὸ τοῦ μνημείου, [3] εἰσελθοῦσαι δὲ οὐχ εὗρον τὸ σῶμα [τοῦ Κυρίου Ἰησοῦ]. [4] καὶ ἐγένετο (ἐν τῷ) ἀπορεῖσθαι αὐτὰς περὶ τούτου καὶ ἰδοὺ (ἄνδρες) δύο (ἐπέστησαν) αὐταῖς, ἐν ἐσθῆτι ἀστραπτούσῃ. [5] ἐμφόβων δὲ γενομένων αὐτῶν καὶ (κλινουσῶν) τὰ πρόσωπα εἰς τὴν γῆν, (εἶπαν πρὸς) αὐτάς, Τί ζητεῖτε τὸν ζῶντα μετὰ τῶν νεκρῶν; [6] [οὐκ ἔστιν ὧδε, ἀλλὰ ἠγέρθη.] (μνήσθητε) ὡς ἐλάλησεν ὑμῖν ἔτι ὢν ἐν τῇ Γαλιλαίᾳ, [7] λέγων τὸν Υἱὸν τοῦ ἀνθρώπου ὅτι δεῖ παραδοθῆναι εἰς χεῖρας ἀνθρώπων ἁμαρτωλῶν καὶ σταυρωθῆναι καὶ τῇ τρίτῃ ἡμέρᾳ ἀναστῆναι. [8] καὶ (ἐμνήσθησαν) (τῶν ῥημάτων) αὐτοῦ, [9] καὶ (ὑποστρέψασαι) [ἀπὸ τοῦ μνημείου] ἀπήγγειλαν ταῦτα

πάντα τοῖς ἕνδεκα καὶ πᾶσιν τοῖς λοιποῖς. [10] ἦσαν δὲ ἡ Μαγδα-
ληνὴ Μαρία καὶ 'Ιωάννα καὶ Μαρία ἡ 'Ιακώβου· καὶ αἱ λοιπαὶ (σὺν)
αὐταῖς (ἔλεγον πρὸς) τοὺς (ἀποστόλους) ταῦτα. [11] καὶ
ἐφάνησαν (ἐνώπιον) αὐτῶν (ὡσεὶ) λῆρος τὰ (ῥήματα) ταῦτα,
καὶ ἠπίστουν αὐταῖς.

Note. The words and phrases common to Luke and Mark, in whole or in
part, are underlined. Those characteristic of Luke listed by Hawkins are
enclosed in rounded brackets, and those claimed by Rehkopf are spaced.
The following are absent from D and important Old Latin MSS and are
indicated by square brackets: (1) τοῦ κυρίου 'Ιησοῦ (v. 3), (2) οὐκ ἔστιν ὧδε,
ἀλλὰ ἠγέρθη (v. 6), (3) ἀπὸ τοῦ μνημείου (v. 9). Verse 12, which is absent
from the same group of MSS, is omitted.

The determining of the source or sources used by Luke in this
narrative is one of unusual difficulty. It is for this reason that
words and phrases are classified as indicated above.

In *BTG*[1] I claimed that the narrative is non-Markan and that
verse 10*a*, 'Now they were Mary Magdalene and Joanna and
Mary the mother of James', is inserted from Mark in it, Salome
(Mark) being replaced by Joanna (cf. Lk. viii. 3). After fuller consideration I believe that this hypothesis is substantially correct,
with some uncertainty regarding vv. 1–3. The earlier investigation was based on statistical, linguistic, and critical grounds, but
these need to be examined and assessed again.

Common words and phrases

Out of 163 words only thirty-seven are common to Luke and
Mark, and if we omit the three phrases which are textually
suspect, the number sinks to thirty, or 19.7 per cent. This
percentage is unusually low, and suggests that substantially the
narrative is non-Markan in origin.

The linguistic facts

Lukan words and constructions are numerous. Hawkins lists the
following: ἐν τῷ *c. infin.*, ἀνήρ, ἐφίστημι, κλίνω, εἶπαν πρός
c. acc., μιμνήσκομαι (twice), ὑποστρέφω, σύν, ἔλεγον πρός *c. acc.*,
ὡσεί, ἀπόστολος, ἐνώπιον, and ῥῆμα (twice). In addition the
narrative contains words and phrases well represented in Luke,
μὲν...δέ, καὶ ἐγένετο...καί, and the two genitive absolutes in v. 5;
or found mainly in Luke/Acts, ἀστράπτω xvii. 24**, ἔμφοβος

[1] Pp. 63–6.

xxiv. 37; Acts x. 4; xxiv. 25; Rev. xi. 13**, ἀπαγγέλλω Luke (11 times), Acts (16), οἱ ἕνδεκα xxiv. 33; Acts i. 26; ii. 14; Matt. xxviii. 16**, ἐσθής Luke (2), Acts (2), Jas. (3)**. This evidence strongly supports the numerical argument.

Subject-matter

The substance of the two narratives in Luke and Mark varies considerably. They agree as to the time and purpose of the visit and in stating that the women found the gravestone rolled away, but in little else. In Luke there is no questioning about who should roll the stone away, and Mark has no parallel to the statement that the women 'found not the body' and 'were perplexed thereabout'. In Mark they see 'a young man sitting on the right side, arrayed in a white robe'. In Luke 'two men stood by them in dazzling apparel' who appear suddenly and apparently are angelic beings (cf. Jn. xx. 12). The effect upon the women is differently described. Whereas in Mark they are 'amazed', in Luke they are 'affrighted' and bow down their faces to the earth. The greatest difference of all is in the account of the words spoken to the women. In Mark the young man commissions them to tell the disciples and Peter that Jesus is risen and will go before them into Galilee where they will see him as he had said. In Luke the heavenly visitors remind them of what he had said 'when he was yet in Galilee' about the delivering up, crucifixion, and resurrection on the third day of the Son of Man. In view of the fidelity with which Luke records sayings in his sources, it is difficult to believe that he has transformed the *Markan* message in this drastic way. Further, while Mark says 'they said nothing to any one', Luke says they 'told all these things to the Eleven, and all the rest'. Similarly, Matthew says they delivered the message to the disciples 'with fear and great joy'. The complete difference in the accounts of the saying suggests that in them we have to do with a separate tradition rather than a reinterpretation of Mark.

It must be conceded, I think, that the case for regarding Lk. xxiv. 1–11 as an independent narrative derived from a non-Markan source, 10a being a Markan insertion, is strong. There is some linguistic evidence pointing to such a source. Rehkopf's list includes ὁ κύριος, κατὰ τὴν ἐντολήν, μιμνήσκομαι, and ἀπόστολος, but the inclusion of ἀπόστολος is doubtful, since

Luke has it twenty-eight times in Acts, and ὁ κύριος is textually uncertain.[1] These items are only faint pointers to a source, since they are small in extent and there are so many 'Lukan' features in the narrative. With reference to the two angelic beings in contrast to Mark's description of a young man in a white robe sitting on the right side, Kirsopp Lake writes, 'Here, then, we have for the first time in Luke a probable trace of knowledge of a tradition not identical with Mark, and of alterations which seem to point to something more than the ordinary desire of a redactor to explain his source.'[2]

Nevertheless, and in spite of what has been said, before the non-Markan character of Lk. xxiv. 1–11 can be accepted with confidence it is necessary to examine the widely accepted view that the Lukan narrative is an edited version of Mk. xvi. 1–8. The situation in Lk. xxiv. 1–3 differs from that which exists in Lk. xxiv. 4–11 and for that reason the two sections must be treated separately. In the former section the problem is mainly numerical; in the latter it is predominantly a question of the subject-matter.

Lk. xxiv. 1–3

Here out of thirty-seven words fifteen are common to Luke and Mark (40 per cent). Luke states that 'on the first day of the week' at early dawn the women came to the tomb bringing the spices they had prepared, that they found the stone rolled away, and that entering in they found not the body (of the Lord Jesus). Luke has not previously mentioned the stone, and it does seem either that he is editing Mark or to some degree reflects a knowledge of Mark. But there is much to be said on the other side. Taken by themselves the 'common' words can be explained without affirming their Markan origin. B. Weiss[3] says that v. 2 (the reference to the stone) *can* only be a reminiscence of Mk. xvi. 3f., but it could be derived from oral tradition. Weiss also says that ἦλθον ἐπί in v. 1 is no reminiscence of Mark, and he appeals to Lk. xix. 5 and xxiii. 33. The phrase ἃ ἡτοίμασαν ἀρώματα points back to Lk. xxiii. 56, ἡτοίμασαν ἀρώματα, and ἡ μία τῶν σαββάτων was probably established in Christian usage from a very early date (cf. Acts xx. 7). Verse 3 has

---

[1] See the Note above, p. 104.

[2] *The Historical Evidence for the Resurrection of Jesus Christ*, p. 67.

[3] *Die Evangelien des Markus und Lukas* (in Meyer's *Commentary*), p. 677.

only a single word in common with Mark and, in contrast with Mark, states that the women did not find the body. A case therefore can be made out for the view that vv. 1–3 are non-Markan. Nevertheless, while the 'common' words and phrases can be accounted for individually, it is significant that so many of them appear in the short space of three verses. Considered as a whole they suggest that in some way yet to be determined a knowledge of Mk. xvi. 1–5 is presupposed.

Lk. xxiv. 4–11

The numerical evidence does not support the view that this section is based on Mark, for, if we omit the two phrases which are textually doubtful, only fourteen out of 115 words (12.2 per cent) are common to Luke and Mark, and seven of these appear in v. 10a. The problem of the origin of the section depends, therefore, on the subject-matter. Three questions arise when Luke's narrative is compared with Mk. xvi. 5–8: (a) Luke's treatment of the Markan reference to the young man clothed in a white robe, (b) his attitude to the message that Jesus will go before the disciples into *Galilee* where they will see him, (c) his statement that the women reported what had happened to the Eleven in contrast to Mark's declaration that they said nothing to any one. The vital question is, 'Does Luke's narrative imply that he dissents from the Markan statements and that he edits Mk. xvi. 5–8 drastically or, on the contrary, that his source is not Mark but a non-Markan tradition?'

(a) It is at least possible that Luke took exception to Mark's use of νεανίσκος, for elsewhere (Lk. vii. 14; Acts ii. 17; v. 10; xxiii. 18, 22) he uses the word of human beings. But the addition of the phrase περιβεβλημένον στολὴν λευκήν shows that a divine being is meant (cf. Rev. vii. 9, 13) and Luke himself has ἄνδρες δύο. He employs the same phrase when describing heavenly beings in ix. 30 (the transfiguration narrative) and in Acts i. 1–10 (the account of the ascension). It is preferable therefore to suppose that he is using a non-Markan source.

(b) The same alternative view is to be preferred in Luke's account of the angelic message. It can be argued that, since all his resurrection narratives are located in *Jerusalem* and its environs in Lk. xxiv and Acts i. 6–11, he took exception to Mark's statement of the message, 'Go, tell his disciples and Peter, he goes before you into *Galilee*: there shall you see him, as he said unto you', but it does not follow that he is editing Mark in xxiv. 7. It may be that he is drawing upon an independent tradition.

(*c*) Similarly, in his statement that the women 'told all these things to the Eleven' it is unnecessary to suppose that he is contradicting Mark, a hypothesis without adequate support in his use of that source. It is preferable again to conclude that he is reproducing non-Markan tradition.

In all three cases the suggestion of an edited version of Mk. xvi. 5–8 fails. The presentation of the subject-matter supports the conclusion suggested by the linguistic evidence; a non-Markan source is implied. This conclusion necessarily affects our judgement of the origin of vv. 1–3.

Summary

It would appear that, with some hesitation as regards vv. 1–3, numerical and linguistic arguments as well as differences in the subject-matter suggest that the whole of Lk. xxiv. 1–11 is non-Markan with a Markan insertion giving the names of the women in v. 10*a*. The fact that 'Lukanisms' are numerous and the signs of a source few suggests that here, as in xxiii. 55–6*a*, Luke himself has considerably rewritten the material derived from his special source. The double reference to the announcement of the women, to the Eleven in v. 9 and to the Apostles in v. 10*b*, is strange and may be a sign of the fusion of two separate traditions. It is possible that v. 10*b* implies that it was the rest of the women, and not the three named, who gave the message. If the case for dependence on Mark in vv. 1–3 were stronger, we should conclude that Luke has combined Mark's account with a non-Markan source in vv. 4–11, but the linguistic evidence does not require this hypothesis, and it is better to infer that Luke shows a knowledge of Mark in vv. 1–3, as apparently he does in xxii. 47, 69, 71. In this case the Markan contacts belong to the stage when the Third Gospel was compiled.

The text of xxiv. 10

Some MSS (Θ *et al.*) read αἵ before ἔλεγον. So the Textus Receptus. Cf. NEB, 'The women were Mary of Magdala,

Joanna, and Mary the mother of James, and they, with the other women, told the apostles.'[1] But the textual evidence does not support this smooth rendering. In both WH and Nestle the subject of ἔλεγον is αἱ λοιπαί.

Implications

If Lk. xxiv. 1–11 is an edited version of Mark it would follow that Lk. xxiv. 1–53 was added at the time when the Third Gospel was compiled, and, further, that the special source ended with the centurion's confession and the return of the people to Jerusalem. This is a possible view to take, for we have seen[2] that apparently at one time a Passion source existed which began with the arrest and ended with the centurion's confession. But we have also seen[3] that in Luke's special source the summary version of the agony serves to combine this account with the section on the Supper and the conversations that followed (Lk. xxii. 14–38). Moreover, it is difficult to believe that the special source contained no reference to the resurrection. The fact that several stories in the special source reveal a knowledge of Mark, including Lk. xxiv. 1–3, may well be explained as modifications in the source made by the evangelist at the time when he gave its final form to the Gospel. The same explanation applies to the passages, such as Lk. xxiii. 55–6a and xxiv. 1–11, in which 'Lukanisms' abound.

20. THE JOURNEY TO EMMAUS

(Lk. xxiv. 13–35)[4]

[13] Καὶ ἰδοὺ δύο ἐξ αὐτῶν ἐν αὐτῇ τῇ ἡμέρᾳ ἦσαν πορευόμενοι εἰς κώμην ἀπέχουσαν σταδίους ἑξήκοντα ἀπὸ Ἰερουσαλήμ, ᾗ

---

[1] RSV reads: 'Now it was Mary Magdalene and Joanna and Mary the mother of James and the other women with them who told this to the apostles.'

[2] See above, pp. 70–2. [3] *Ibid.*

[4] This narrative is found only in Luke, and there are no Markan insertions or additions. The question at issue is whether it is a free composition on the part of Luke or whether he has drawn upon a source. It will prove useful to underline significant words and constructions found elsewhere in Luke and Acts, to enclose those characteristic of Luke according to Hawkins in brackets, and to indicate words and phrases included in Rehkopf's list by letter-spacing.

(ὄνομα) Ἐμμαοῦς, [14] (καὶ αὐτοὶ) ὡμίλουν (πρὸς ἀλλήλους) περὶ πάντων τῶν συμβεβηκότων τούτων. [15] καὶ ἐγένετο (ἐν τῷ) ὁμιλεῖν αὐτοὺς καὶ συνζητεῖν, (καὶ αὐτὸς) Ἰησοῦς ἐγγίσας συνεπορεύετο αὐτοῖς· [16] οἱ δὲ ὀφθαλμοὶ αὐτῶν ἐκρατοῦντο (τοῦ) μὴ ἐπιγνῶναι αὐτόν. [17] (εἶπεν δὲ πρὸς αὐτούς), Τίνες οἱ λόγοι οὗτοι οὓς ἀντιβάλλετε (πρὸς ἀλλήλους) περιπατοῦντες; καὶ ἐστάθησαν σκυθρωποί. [18] ἀποκριθεὶς δὲ εἷς (ὀνόματι) Κλεοπᾶς (εἶπεν πρὸς αὐτόν), Σὺ μόνος παροικεῖς Ἰερουσαλήμ καὶ οὐκ ἔγνως τὰ γενόμενα ἐν αὐτῇ (ἐν ταῖς ἡμέραις ταύταις); [19] καὶ εἶπεν αὐτοῖς, Ποῖα; οἱ δὲ εἶπαν αὐτῷ, Τὰ περὶ Ἰησοῦ τοῦ Ναζαρηνοῦ, ὃς ἐγένετο (ἀνὴρ) προφήτης δυνατὸς ἐν ἔργῳ καὶ λόγῳ ἐναντίον τοῦ Θεοῦ καὶ (παντὸς τοῦ λαοῦ), [20] ὅπως (τε) παρέδωκαν αὐτὸν οἱ ἀρχιερεῖς καὶ (οἱ ἄρχοντες) ἡμῶν εἰς κρίμα θανάτου καὶ ἐσταύρωσαν αὐτόν. [21] ἡμεῖς δὲ ἠλπίζομεν ὅτι αὐτός ἐστιν ὁ μέλλων λυτροῦσθαι τὸν Ἰσραήλ· ἀλλά (γε) καὶ (σὺν) πᾶσιν τούτοις τρίτην ταύτην ἡμέραν (ἄγει) ἀφ᾽ οὗ ταῦτα ἐγένετο. [22] ἀλλὰ καὶ γυναῖκές (τινες) ἐξ ἡμῶν ἐξέστησαν ἡμᾶς, (γενόμεναι ὀρθριναὶ ἐπὶ) τὸ μνημεῖον, [23] καὶ μὴ εὑροῦσαι τὸ σῶμα αὐτοῦ ἦλθον λέγουσαι καὶ ὀπτασίαν ἀγγέλων ἑωρακέναι, οἳ λέγουσιν αὐτὸν ζῆν. [24] καὶ ἀπῆλθόν τινες τῶν (σὺν) ἡμῖν ἐπὶ τὸ μνημεῖον, καὶ εὗρον οὕτως καθὼς καὶ αἱ γυναῖκες εἶπον, αὐτὸν δὲ οὐκ εἶδον. [25] (καὶ αὐτὸς) (εἶπεν πρὸς αὐτούς), Ὦ ἀνόητοι καὶ βραδεῖς τῇ καρδίᾳ (τοῦ) πιστεύειν ἐπὶ πᾶσιν (οἷς) ἐλάλησαν οἱ προφῆται· [26] οὐχὶ ταῦτα ἔδει παθεῖν τὸν Χριστὸν καὶ εἰσελθεῖν εἰς τὴν δόξαν αὐτοῦ; [27] καὶ ἀρξάμενος ἀπὸ Μωϋσέως καὶ ἀπὸ πάντων τῶν προφητῶν διερμήνευσεν αὐτοῖς ἐν πάσαις ταῖς γραφαῖς (τὰ περὶ) ἑαυτοῦ. [28] Καὶ ἤγγισαν εἰς τὴν κώμην (οὗ) ἐπορεύοντο, (καὶ αὐτὸς) προσεποιήσατο πορρώτερον πορεύεσθαι. [29] καὶ παρεβιάσαντο αὐτὸν λέγοντες, Μεῖνον μεθ᾽ ἡμῶν, ὅτι πρὸς ἑσπέραν ἐστὶν καὶ (κέκλικεν) ἤδη ἡ ἡμέρα. καὶ εἰσῆλθεν (τοῦ) μεῖναι (σὺν) αὐτοῖς. [30] καὶ ἐγένετο ἐν τῷ (κατακλιθῆναι) αὐτὸν μετ᾽ αὐτῶν λαβὼν τὸν ἄρτον εὐλόγησεν καὶ κλάσας (ἐπεδίδου) αὐτοῖς· [31] αὐτῶν δὲ (διηνοίχθησαν) οἱ ὀφθαλμοί, καὶ ἐπέγνωσαν αὐτόν· (καὶ αὐτὸς) ἄφαντος ἐγένετο ἀπ᾽ αὐτῶν. [32] καὶ (εἶπαν πρὸς ἀλλήλους), Οὐχὶ ἡ καρδία ἡμῶν καιόμενη ἦν ἐν ἡμῖν (ὡς) ἐλάλει ἡμῖν ἐν τῇ ὁδῷ, (ὡς) (διήνοιγεν) ἡμῖν τὰς γραφάς; [33] Καὶ (ἀναστάντες) αὐτῇ τῇ ὥρᾳ (ὑπέστρε-ψαν) εἰς Ἰερουσαλήμ, καὶ εὗρον ἠθροισμένους τοὺς ἕνδεκα καὶ τοὺς (σὺν) αὐτοῖς, [34] λέγοντας ὅτι ὄντως ἠγέρθη ὁ Κύριος καὶ ὤφθη Σίμωνι. [35] (καὶ αὐτοὶ) ἐξηγοῦντο (τὰ ἐν) τῇ ὁδῷ καὶ ὡς ἐγνώσθη αὐτοῖς ἐν τῇ κλάσει τοῦ ἄρτου.

It will be seen that Luke's responsibility for the diction of the narrative is very considerable. The forty-three instances of words and phrases from Hawkins's list speak for themselves and the remaining words underlined, found in most cases in Luke and Acts, point to the same conclusion. Stanton has listed many examples of Luke's style,[1] and includes the narrative among the nine sections 'whose literary form should in all probability be attributed solely to the author himself of the third Gospel and Acts'.

Among the instances Stanton suggests are two cases of the periphrastic imperfect (vv. 13 and 32), two of the construction καὶ ἐγένετο ἐν τῷ c. infin. (vv. 15 and 30), several verbs compounded with σύν, the construction of vv. 22f., δυνατὸς ἐν ἔργῳ καὶ λόγῳ, cf. Acts vii. 22, and verbs including ἀπέχω ἀπό, ἐξίστημι, διερμηνεύω, διανοίγω, ἀθροίζω, the forensic use of κρίμα, and ὀρθρινός. To these may be added the following additional examples: καὶ ἰδού (v. 13), Ἰερουσαλήμ (vv. 13, 18, 33), ὁμιλέω (v. 14f.; Acts xx. 11, xxiv. 26**), τὰ γενόμενα (v. 18), παραβιάζομαι (v. 29; cf. Acts xvi. 15**), οἱ ἕνδεκα (v. 33), αὐτῇ τῇ ὥρᾳ (v. 33).[2] All these mount up to an impressive total. The evidence supplied by the vocabulary, syntax, and style strongly suggests that the evangelist has composed the narrative. The possibility, however, that he has embellished existing tradition is not excluded, although signs of an older source are few. Words and phrases included in Rehkopf's

---

[1] GHD, ii, 308ff.
[2] Cf. M. Black, An Aramaic Approach to the Gospels and Acts[3], pp. 108–12. Note also ἀρξάμενος ἀπό (cf. xxiii. 5) in xxiv. 27. On this see p. 87 above.

list are ἀπέχω (v. 13), καὶ αὐτοί (v. 14), εἶπεν *c. dat.* (twice in v. 19), ἀφ' οὗ (v. 21), ἐγγίζω (vv. 15, 28), ἤδη (v. 29), ὁ Κύριος (v. 34); that is, nine in twenty-three verses. This small total is due to the large extent to which Luke's diction appears in the narrative. His vivid portraiture is present in the dialogue between Jesus and Cleopas and his companion, and the story is linked to the account of the visit of the women to the tomb by the phrase 'that very day' in v. 13 and by the declaration of the angels who said that Jesus was alive (v. 23). The slowness of the two travellers to believe is described in vv. 21-5, and the appeal to the Scriptures is characteristically Lukan. Unlike most Synoptic stories the narrative consists of three parts or scenes: the journey, the meal at Emmaus, and the return to Jerusalem. In each case the scene is skilfully depicted, especially the recognition and vanishing of Jesus in the second scene. The whole is the work of an artist in words.

Summary

In this narrative the vocabulary, syntax, and style suggest that Luke has embellished an existing tradition with unusual freedom and possibly has expanded an earlier source.[1]

21. THE APPEARANCE TO THE ELEVEN

(Lk. xxiv. 36-49)

[36] Ταῦτα δὲ αὐτῶν λαλούντων αὐτὸς ἔστη ἐν μέσῳ αὐτῶν. [37] πτοηθέντες δὲ καὶ ἔμφοβοι γενόμενοι ἐδόκουν πνεῦμα θεωρεῖν. [38] καὶ εἶπεν αὐτοῖς· τί τεταραγμένοι ἐστέ, καὶ διὰ τί (διαλογισμοὶ) ἀναβαίνουσιν ἐν τῇ καρδίᾳ ὑμῶν; [39] ἴδετε τὰς χεῖράς μου καὶ τοὺς πόδας μου, ὅτι ἐγώ εἰμι αὐτός· ψηλαφήσατέ με καὶ ἴδετε, ὅτι πνεῦμα σάρκα καὶ ὀστέα οὐκ ἔχει καθὼς ἐμὲ θεωρεῖτε ἔχοντα. [[40] καὶ τοῦτο εἰπὼν ἔδειξεν αὐτοῖς τὰς χεῖρας καὶ τοὺς πόδας.] [41] ἔτι δὲ ἀπιστούντων αὐτῶν ἀπὸ τῆς χαρᾶς καὶ θαυμαζόντων, εἶπεν αὐτοῖς· ἔχετέ τι βρώσιμον ἐνθάδε; [42] οἱ

---

[1] F. Hahn, *Christologische Hoheitstitel*, p. 387, maintains that xxiv. 13-35 certainly contains an old nucleus which in its present setting has been expanded by the addition of vv. 33-5 and all the elements connected with it in vv. 14, 15*a*, 17-27, and 32.

δὲ (ἐπέδωκαν) αὐτῷ ἰχθύος ὀπτοῦ μέρος· [43] καὶ λαβὼν (ἐνώπιον) αὐτῶν ἔφαγεν. [44] (Εἶπεν δὲ πρὸς αὐτούς)· οὗτοι οἱ
λόγοι μου οὓς (ἐλάλησα πρὸς ὑμᾶς) ἔτι ὢν (σὺν) ὑμῖν, ὅτι δεῖ
πληρωθῆναι πάντα τὰ γεγραμμένα ἐν τῷ νόμῳ Μωϋσέως καὶ τοῖς
προφήταις καὶ ψαλμοῖς περὶ ἐμοῦ. [45] τότε (διήνοιξεν) αὐτῶν
τὸν νοῦν τοῦ (συν)ιέναι τὰς γραφάς· [46] καὶ εἶπεν αὐτοῖς ὅτι
οὕτως γέγραπται παθεῖν τὸν Χριστὸν καὶ ἀναστῆναι ἐκ νεκρῶν
τῇ τρίτῃ ἡμέρᾳ, [47] καὶ κηρυχθῆναι ἐπὶ τῷ ὀνόματι αὐτοῦ
μετάνοιαν εἰς ἄφεσιν ἁμαρτιῶν εἰς πάντα τὰ ἔθνη, — ἀρξάμενοι
ἀπὸ Ἰερουσαλήμ. [48] ὑμεῖς μάρτυρες τούτων. [49] καὶ ἰδοὺ ἐγὼ
(ἐξαποστέλλω) τὴν ἐπαγγελίαν τοῦ πατρός μου ἐφ᾽ ὑμᾶς· ὑμεῖς
δὲ καθίσατε ἐν τῇ πόλει ἕως οὗ ἐνδύσησθε ἐξ ὕψους δύναμιν.

Note. Like the preceding narrative this account is peculiar to Luke and
there are no Markan insertions and additions. Words and constructions
found elsewhere in Luke and Acts are underlined, those characteristic of
Luke bracketed, and those in Rehkopf's list letter-spaced.

Again, Stanton's judgement regarding the narrative is confirmed,
but proportionately to its length the signs of Luke's diction are
fewer, and there is greater reason to presume that he is using a
source. Rehkopf's list offers little support for this inference (there
are only the three examples of εἶπεν *c. dat.*). Applying the principles of form-criticism C. H. Dodd has shown that its structure
conforms to that of the 'concise' narratives (Class I) in the
resurrection tradition.[1] The pattern, he points out, has been
extensively worked over and has become a piece of controversial
apologetic. The process of recognition is greatly spun out. The
disciples are terrified and think they are seeing a ghost. Jesus
points to his hands and feet (cf. Jn. xx. 20), invites them to touch
him (cf. Jn. xx. 27) and eats in their presence, and the concluding
word of command is replaced by an address.[2] Dodd writes: 'It
is certainly more remote from the original tradition, orally
handed down, than the typical narratives of Class I, but the
obvious work of an author has not altogether disguised the
form of the tradition which underlies.'[3]

[1] *Studies in the Gospels* (ed. D. E. Nineham), pp. 16–18. See above, p. 36.
[2] The greeting appears only if καὶ λέγει αὐτοῖς· εἰρήνη ὑμῖν is read in v. 36.
This reading, like that in v. 40, is probably an assimilation to Jn. xx. 19f.,
26. [3] *Op. cit.* p. 18.

The hand of the author is not difficult to detect. It appears in the apologetic motive which emphasises the material aspects of the resurrection – in the invitation to handle the limbs of the risen Christ and the reference to his eating of a piece of cooked fish. Doctrinal interests are also present in the allusion to the teaching of Scripture that the Messiah is to suffer death and to rise on the third day, and in the command to await the promised gift of the Spirit in Jerusalem. While, however, these are ideas congenial to Luke, in presenting them he is only underlining beliefs present in the primitive tradition.

The linguistic facts suggest that Luke is developing an existing source. There are nine examples, indicated above by brackets, of his characteristic words and phrases. Stanton draws attention to other supporting phenomena.[1] πτοεῖσθαι, he points out, occurs elsewhere only in Lk. xxi. 9, and for ἔμφοβοι he refers us to xxiv. 5. ἀναβαίνω is used in a figurative sense as in Acts vii. 23 and 1 Cor. ii. 9 (but in both cases with ἐπί). With παθεῖν τὸν Χριστόν he compares Lk. xxiv. 26, and with ἐπὶ τῷ ὀνόματι... ἁμαρτιῶν Acts ii. 38. He cites a parallel in Acts i. 8b to εἰς πάντα τὰ ἔθνη – ἀρξάμενοι ἀπὸ[2] Ἰερουσαλήμ. ὑμεῖς μάρτυρες τούτων, and to the promise of the Holy Spirit and power in v. 49 he relates the similar passages in Acts i. 4 and 8a. These correspondences with the narrative of Acts i. 1–8 strengthen the case for affirming an identity of authorship in Lk. xxiv. 36–49. To Stanton's examples may be added the three cases of the genitive absolute in vv. 36 and 41, the record of ψηλαφάω (elsewhere only in Acts xvii. 27; Heb. xii. 18, and 1 Jn. i. 1), and the parallel to ἀπὸ τῆς χαρᾶς (v. 41) in Acts xii. 14 and Lk. xxiv. 52.

Summary

On critical and linguistic grounds we are justified in concluding that the account of the appearance to the Eleven is to be explained as Luke's embellishment of an earlier source.

22. THE ASCENSION (Lk. xxiv. 50–3)

[50] Ἐξήγαγεν δὲ αὐτοὺς ἕως πρὸς Βηθανίαν, καὶ (ἐπάρας) τὰς χεῖρας αὐτοῦ εὐλόγησεν αὐτούς, [51] καὶ ἐγένετο ἐν τῷ εὐλογεῖν

---

[1] *GHD*, II, 309.
[2] See the note on ἀρξάμενος ἀπό in xxiii. 5, p. 87 above.

αὐτὸν αὐτοὺς διέστη ἀπ' αὐτῶν [καὶ ἀνεφέρετο εἰς τὸν οὐρανόν].
[52] (καὶ αὐτοὶ) (ὑπέστρεψαν) εἰς Ἰερουσαλήμ μετὰ χαρᾶς
μεγάλης, [53] καὶ ἦσαν διὰ παντὸς ἐν τῷ ἱερῷ εὐλογοῦντες τὸν
θεόν.

Note. The narrative is peculiar to Luke, and there are no Markan insertions.
Words and phrases characteristic of Luke are enclosed in round brackets,
and these and other words found in Luke and Acts are underlined. There
are no words or phrases listed by Rehkopf.

The sentence in v. 51, omitted by ℵ* D a b e ff² j l (sy⁵), is enclosed in
square brackets, but should probably be read (cf. Streeter, *FG*, pp. 142f.,
408).

The diction of this short narrative is distinctively Lukan. There
are three words or phrases characteristic of Luke, according to
Hawkins (ἐπαίρω, καὶ αὐτοί, and ὑποστρέφω), and several
words common to Luke and Acts. Stanton[1] instances the parallel
to ὑπέστρεψαν εἰς Ἰερουσαλήμ in Acts i. 12, the use of διΐστημι
in Lk. xxii. 59, and of διὰ παντός in Acts ii. 25 (LXX); x. 2. In
addition, two frequently used constructions in Luke (καὶ
ἐγένετο and ἐν τῷ *c. acc.* and *infin.*) appear in v. 51.[2] The form
Ἰερουσαλήμ once more stands in v. 52 and the Lukan emphasis on
joy is found in μετὰ χαρᾶς (cf. xxiv. 41; Acts xii. 14). There is
also ἐξάγω (v. 50*, Acts (8)*). οὐρανός is used in the singular
as frequently in Luke/Acts.

The narrative forms a climax to the resurrection stories of xxiv.
This is implied by αὐτούς = 'the Eleven', and the references to
parting and the return to Jerusalem.

Summary

The narrative is the composition of the evangelist. He may be
adapting a source, although this is not indicated by the diction.
Stanton[3] observes, 'There are many of his characteristic expressions [in xxiv] and the closing verses are closely connected with
and parallel to the opening passage of the Acts.'

[1] *GHD*, ii, 309.
[2] Cf. Moulton–Howard, *Grammar*, ii, 450f.
[3] *GHD*, ii, 309.

PART THREE

THE SPECIAL LUKAN PASSION
NARRATIVE

I. SUMMARY AND CONCLUSIONS

In the foregoing investigation it has been claimed that, with the exception of Lk. xxii. 1–13 and 54*b*–61 (the denial) and xxiii. 50–4 (the burial), together with 'Markan insertions' and 'additions', and other additions and modifications introduced by Luke himself when he composed the Gospel, the Lukan narratives of the Passion and resurrection were probably derived from an earlier non-Markan source or sources. The words 'insertions' and 'additions' are used provisionally, but it is claimed that such appears to be their character in relation to the narratives in which they stand. A few passages[1] are partially assimilated to Mark. These passages can be adequately explained as influenced by a knowledge of Mark at the time when the Third Gospel was compiled. How far they imply a knowledge of Mark is an open question; they are mentioned in order to include as much as possible in assessing the Markan element in xxii–xxiv. If they were more numerous, we should have to abandon the hypothesis of a special non-Markan Passion and resurrection source, or at least to render it doubtful and uncertain, but there can be no valid objection to the possibility that, when Luke used Mark, he carried over from this Gospel words and phrases in the passages in question. Indeed, in the process of compilation it would be strange if he had not done so, and we must accept the fact that in these cases we cannot recover with any certainty the original text of the special source.

The Markan element in Luke includes: xxii. 1–13, 22, 34, 46*b*, 50*b*, 52*b*–53*a*, 54*b*–61; xxiii. 3, 26, 34*b*, 38, 44f., 49, 50–4; xxiv. 10*a*. Passages which appear to reflect the influence of Mark are: xxii. 47, 69, 71; xxiv. 1–3.

---

[1] See above, p. 33; cf. my article 'Methods of Gospel Criticism', ET, LXXI, 69, and *The Gospels* (9th ed.), p. 43. After repeated study I have decided to omit xxii. 39 and 66, and xxiii. 33. Streeter listed xxii. 69; xxiii. 35, 49, 51; xxiv. 1–3, 9f. as possibly Markan or partially assimilated to the Markan parallel. Cf. *FG*, p. 222.

It is necessary now to examine the literary phenomena as a whole in relation to the following questions:[1]

(*a*) Does the evidence point to separate non-Markan sources or to one continuous non-Markan source?

(*b*) If the latter, was the source oral, or

(*c*) was it documentary?

(*d*) Was the source limited to the Passion and resurrection, or was it part of a larger entity (Proto-Luke) dealing with the gospel story?

(*e*) Can we determine the authorship of the source and the approximate date of its composition?

(*a*) Reasons for thinking of a single non-Markan source rather than of separate non-Markan sources

We have found reason to think that (*a*) Lk. xxii. 14–38 (less Markan insertions) and (*b*) a Passion narrative beginning with the arrest and ending with the centurion's confession existed at one time as separate entities, and also that there were stages in the composition of xxii. 14–38, but these views are speculative, and the probability is that the whole of xxii. 14 – xxiv. 53 (less Markan insertions and additions and other additions and modifications introduced by Luke himself when he composed the Gospel) formed a Passion and resurrection source before the composition of the Third Gospel. Several reasons suggest this conclusion.

(1) In the first place, the continuity of the non-Markan narratives is of such a kind that when we exclude passages of Markan origin, we are left with a story which can be read as a whole. The only gaps are at the beginning, where no explanation of the 'hour' mentioned in xxii. 14 is given, and at the end, where no reference to the burial is supplied. These gaps, however, are not fatal to the hypothesis of a non-Markan source. It is reasonable to suppose that the original beginning has been replaced by the Markan section in xxii. 1–13, and to infer that the Markan burial story in xxiii. 50–4 may have cancelled a reference to the tomb in the original source. For the rest, from the account of the Last Supper onwards, the narrative moves with such ease and

---

[1] These were the questions discussed in *BTG*, pp. 68–75. They need to be considered again in the light of the preceding investigation.

vigour that it is difficult to think of it as any other than a continuous source.

(2) Secondly, the cross-references and connexions between the several narratives point to the same conclusion. Some of these may have been assimilated to Mark when the Third Gospel was compiled, but examples of this are few and are not inconsistent with the hypothesis of an original source. The account of the Last Supper is combined with the conversations after the institution of the Eucharist, so that Lk. xxii. 14–38 forms a unity. This section is connected with the story of the agony by the words, 'And he came forth, and went, as his custom was, to the mount of Olives', and the story of the betrayal and arrest is introduced by the words, 'While he yet spoke, behold, a crowd, and he that was called Judas, one of the Twelve, went before them.' The arrest, the mocking, and the examination before the priests are firmly linked together, and the trial before Herod is merged into the account of the examination before Pilate. The crucifixion narrative follows naturally, and the account of the action of the women leads on to the story of their visit to the tomb. The journey to Emmaus takes place 'on the same day', and the return to Jerusalem is joined to the appearance to the Eleven by the phrase 'And as they spoke these things'. In short, the Lukan Passion story is a connected whole.

(3) Thirdly, the portraiture of Jesus is the same all the way through. There is the same consistent attitude towards the crowd, to Jews and Gentiles, to the hierarchy, to women, and to sinners. An appeal to Scripture runs throughout. As during the Supper Jesus quotes Isa. liii. 12 with the claim, 'this which is written must be fulfilled in me', so at the examination before the priests he quotes Ps. cx. 1, and in the appearances the risen Christ interprets the 'things concerning himself' from the law, the prophets, and the psalms (cf. xxiv. 27, 44–7). We are fully justified in speaking of a continuous source rather than of separate sources, diverse in origin, which have been strung together. The writer is an author, not a compiler or editor.

(b) Is the source an oral source?

The trend of the investigation is in favour of the view that the source was a document, and this is especially the case if we have correctly understood the use which is made of Mark. We have already seen in Part One that, in agreement with Feine, this was Hawkins's earlier conclusion and was preferred by Sanday.[1] If Rehkopf's hypothesis is accepted, the same conclusion follows. This submission is taken up and carried further in the following section.

(c) Reasons for regarding the source as a document

(1) This conclusion is suggested by the *Markan elements* in Lk. xxii–xxiv. These appear to be 'insertions' and 'additions' in the narratives in which they stand. For example, with the removal of the Markan story of the denial, the reference to the journey to the high priest's house and the account of the mocking come together with an improved sequence, and the same is true when certain Markan passages are abstracted from the narrative of the crucifixion. It is largely the view that the burial story is Markan which explains the consistency with which the description of the action of the women after the crucifixion is narrated. Allowing room for doubt in the case of the shorter passages, Markan details such as the prediction of the denial, the severing of the ear of the high priest's servant, the superscription, the reference to the darkness and the rending of the temple veil, all point to the existence of a written source in which they appear as secondary strata.

(2) A second reason for the same conclusion appears in the *variations of order* in Luke as compared with Mark. A list of no less than twelve of these variations is given by Hawkins,[2] who

---

[1] See above, p. 6.

[2] The prediction of the betrayal precedes the Supper in Mark, but follows it in Luke. The Cup follows the mention of the Bread in Mark, but precedes it in the shorter text in Luke. The saying, 'I will not drink from henceforth', comes after the words of institution in Mark, but before (in the longer text) in Luke. In Mark the woe on the traitor comes after the questionings of the apostles; before in Luke. The prediction of the denial follows the departure from the upper room in Mark, but precedes it in Luke. The denial comes after the trial before the priests in Mark; before in Luke. The mocking comes after the trial before the priests in Mark; before in Luke. The superscription is mentioned before the mocking of the various onlookers in all cases in Mark; after in some cases in Luke. The mockery by the soldiers precedes the crucifixion in Mark, but comes during it in Luke (before in the case of Herod's soldiers). In Mark the rending of the veil follows the death of Jesus; precedes it in Luke. The temporal statement comes before the burial in Mark; after in Luke. The pre-

explains them as the product of memoriter narrative and instruction. 'Such inversions of order', he observes, 'are very much more likely to occur in oral than in documentary transmission.'[1] This is an excellent explanation of the changes in order so long as we explain, with Hawkins, the matter peculiar to Luke in the Passion narrative as the result of 'a long and gradual conflation in the mind' of the evangelist .Hawkins's explanation implies that the evangelist has forgotten the order in which the incidents and sayings in question occur in Mark. We shall find it impossible to accept this assumption not only on grounds of probability, but also because of the phenomena themselves as they appear in the Third Gospel. A better explanation of these inversions of order will be found in the theory that the Lukan Passion narrative is non-Markan with Markan insertions and additions.

Five of the inversions of order[2] are at once explained if the Lukan sequence is that of passages in the non-Markan source. The difference of order is due, not to forgetfulness of Mark, but to preference for another source. More significant are the seven remaining instances,[3] for these appear from our investigation to be 'Markan insertions'. We have increased confidence in regarding them as such when we find that *the same theory which explains them as 'insertions' or 'extracts' also explains them as examples of inversion of order.* The conditions are such that they cannot appear in Luke in the order in which they appear in Mark. They are found in a different sequence because they are inserted in Luke. As later strata, they had to take the place which earlier conditions had left. The variations of order are just what we may expect; not something we have to justify.

paration of the spices and ointments follows the reference to the Sabbath in Mark; precedes it in Luke. The names of the women are given before the visit to the tomb in Mark, but after this incident in Luke. In contrast with Luke, Matthew follows the order of Mark except that he does not mention the preparation of the spices and ointments. See *Oxford Studies*, pp. 81–4; Jeremias, *The Eucharistic Words of Jesus*, pp. 98f.

[1] *Oxford Studies*, p. 84.
[2] The prediction of the betrayal, the mocking, the mockery of the soldiers, the preparation of the spices and ointments, the names of the women.
[3] The Cup (Lk. xx. 19*a*), the woe pronounced on the traitor (xxii. 22), the prediction of the denial (xxii. 34), the denial (xxii. 54*b*–61), the superscription (xxiii. 38), the rending of the temple veil (xxiii. 44f.), the temporal statement regarding the Preparation (xxiii. 54).

(3) A third argument in favour of the existence of a non-Markan documentary source is that, *on this hypothesis, we can show that the evangelist was well alive to the order of Mark.* We have no need to assume what Hawkins describes as 'a long and gradual conflation in the mind'. The order of Mark has not been forgotten; it is very much in mind. For, if a list be made of the passages we have found reason to call 'Markan insertions', it will be seen that they occur in Luke in precisely the same relative order in which they stand in Mark. This will be apparent in the following table:

Markan insertions and additions in Luke	Parallel passages in Mark
xxii. 1–13	xiv. 1f., 10–16
22	21
34	30
46*b*	38
50*b*	47*b*
52*b*–53*a*	48*b*–49
54*b*–61	54, 66–72
xxiii. 3	xv. 2
25	15
26	21
34*b*	24*b*
38	26
44f.	33, 38
49	40
50–4	42–7
xxiv. 10*a*	xvi. 1 (cf. xv. 40)

The table shows that the evangelist has no confused recollection of the sequence of events in Mark; he knows that sequence perfectly well. All the Lukan items in the list follow the Markan order exactly. The passages, xxii. 47, 69, 71, and xxiv. 1–3, which may reflect the influence of Mark linguistically, stand in a different order because of their non-Markan contexts. Lk. xxii. 19*a* may be another case of this kind.[1] We are left with the impression that, coming to the Markan story with his special source in mind, the evangelist has noted features which he desires to incorporate in his Gospel and has introduced these borrowings in their original Markan order at such points as the special source permitted.

---

[1] In *BTG*, pp. 37–40, verse 19*a* was explained as a Markan insertion. See, however, the discussion on pp. 50–8 above.

The order of the 'insertions' supplies strong confirmatory evidence in favour of the provisional conclusions already reached. It supports the view that the Markan passages in Luke are rightly described as 'insertions' and 'additions' and that the non-Markan narratives are parts of an existing document. It is generally agreed that in Lk. iii. 1 – xxi the evangelist follows the order of Mark with remarkable fidelity. On the ordinary theory of the composition of the Gospel, his relation to Mark's order in xxii–xxiv is very different. On the hypothesis maintained in the present study, his procedure is the same all the way through; wherever and however he uses Mark he observes its order.

The above considerations furnish strong reasons for thinking that the substance of Lk. xxii. 14 – xxiv was put together independently of Mark, and that it existed as a document before the evangelist had seen Mark. At a later time he expanded the Passion narrative by inserting extracts from Mark.

(d) Is the source part of a larger whole?

To answer this question a full consideration of the Proto-Luke hypothesis would be necessary. This inquiry cannot be undertaken here, but this much at least may be claimed. The Lukan Passion narrative cannot have begun with xxii. 14 ('And when the hour was come, he sat down, and the apostles with him'). We may also fairly urge the antecedent improbability of a source so rich in historical details, and so evidently resting upon the witness of people in close touch with tradition, being confined to the incidents of the Passion and resurrection. There is good reason to maintain that Lk. xxii. 14 – xxiv is part of a larger whole.

(e) Authorship and date

Here a modification of the results claimed in *BTG* must be made. Rehkopf's results show that the Passion source has a vocabulary and style of its own which is different from those of the Gospel and Acts. The words characteristic of the Gospel are those listed by Hawkins. The speech usage of the special source is not that of the Gospel and Acts. If we set aside examples which appear in Acts only once or twice, only nine appear in Acts with relative frequency. The case for the common authorship of Luke and Acts, especially that connected with the 'We-sections' in Acts, is, in my opinion, well based. But if so, and Luke is the author, he cannot have been the compiler of the special source.[1] Its characteristic ideas are certainly those of Luke and Acts, and for this reason we must infer that Luke found them congenial and perhaps influential in the composition of Luke/Acts. Characteristic Lukan words appear in all the narratives of Lk. xxii. 14ff., and this is especially true of the resurrection stories of Lk. xxiv. While then he uses a written source, Luke's hand is plainly to be seen in these chapters. The probability that he found the source when visiting Caesarea at the time indicated by Acts xxi. 8 still stands, as well as the date of composition A.D. 60–5. Its author is unknown, but, it may be conjectured, probably belonged to the circle connected with Philip the Evangelist and his four prophesying daughters.

2. THE TEXT OF THE PASSION SOURCE

The translation which follows is not intended as a new rendering, but only to display the unity and continuity of the Lukan Passion source. In it the Markan insertions and additions are omitted[2] and passages in which the evangelist's knowledge of Mark is possible are enclosed in brackets.[3] The result is to show that the source is not a mere collection of fragments, but is an account of the Passion and resurrection which forms a literary whole. The source may be a combination of two earlier sections, the Last Supper and the arrest of Jesus with its tragic sequel, connected by the story of the agony; but this suggestion is hypothetical and speculative. It is, however, supported by the agreement in the

---

[1] The words in Rehkopf's list which appear in Acts with relative frequency are: αἰνεῖν (3), ἄξιος (7), ἀπόστολος (28), βαστάζειν (4), κατά = 'according to' (16), φίλος (3), φοβεῖσθαι with God as the object (5), χαίρειν 'to rejoice' (5), and the historical present (13), that is, approximately only one in ten.

[2] The following passages are also omitted for the reasons stated: (a) Lk. xxii. 19–20 as belonging to a pre-Lukan liturgical source distinct from the special Passion source (see pp. 57f. and 68 n. 2). (b) Lk. xxiii. 25 as an addition made by Luke when the Gospel as such was composed (see p. 89). (c) Lk. xxiv. 50–3 as the composition of the evangelist himself (see p. 115) [Ed.].

[3] Passages in which the special source, according to Dr Taylor's investigation, has been considerably re-written or embellished by the evangelist himself are enclosed in square brackets [Ed.].

order of the narratives with that of the Gospel of John. The translation confirms the results obtained by the linguistic and literary
examination of Lk. xxii. 14 – xxiv. 53.

Translation

And when the hour had come he sat down and the apostles with
him. And he said unto them, 'I have earnestly desired to eat this
Passover meal with you before I suffer. For I say unto you that
I will no longer eat it until it is fulfilled in the kingdom of God.'
And receiving a cup he gave thanks and said, 'Take this and
divide it among yourselves, for I say unto you, I will not drink
from henceforth of the fruit of the vine until the kingdom of God
shall come.

'Howbeit behold the hand of him who will betray me is with
me at the table.' And they began to question with one another
who then it might be of them who was about to do this thing.

And there was a contention among them about which of them
might seem to be the greatest. And he said unto them, 'The kings
of the Gentiles lord it over them and those in authority over them
are called "Benefactors". But you shall not be so, but let the
greatest among you be as the youngest, and he that leads as he
that serves. For who is the greater, he who sits at meat or he who
serves? Is it not he who sits at meat? But I am in the midst of you
as he who serves.

'But you are they who have continued with me in my trials.
And I covenant unto you a kingdom as my Father covenanted a
kingdom to me, that you may eat and drink at my table in my
kingdom. And you shall sit on thrones judging the twelve tribes
of Israel.

'Simon, Simon, behold Satan asked to have you that he might
sift you as wheat, but I made supplication for you that your faith
may not fail. And when you have turned again strengthen your
brethren.' And he said unto him, 'Lord, I am ready to go with
you to prison and to death.'

And he said to them, 'When I sent you without purse and
wallet and sandals, did you lack anything?' And they said,
'Nothing.' And he said unto them, 'But now let him who has a
purse take it, and in like manner a wallet, and he who has none
let him sell his cloak and buy a sword. For I say unto you that this
which is written must be fulfilled in my case, "And he was

numbered with lawless men". For my life draws to its end.' And they said, 'Lord, here are two swords.' And he said to them, 'It is enough.'

And he went out and journeyed as his custom was to the Mount of Olives, and the disciples followed him. And when he came to the place he said to them, 'Pray that you do not enter into trial.' And he was parted from them about a stone's cast. And he fell on his knees and prayed saying, 'Father, if it is thy will, remove this cup from me: nevertheless, not my will but thine be done.' And an angel from heaven appeared, strengthening him. And being in an agony he prayed the more earnestly; and his sweat became like drops of blood falling down upon the ground. And he arose from prayer, and when he came to the disciples he found them sleeping for sorrow. And he said to them, 'Why are you sleeping? Arise.'

(And while he was still speaking, behold, there was a crowd, and he that was called Judas, one of the Twelve, went before them. And he came near to Jesus to kiss him.) But Jesus said to him, 'Judas, would you betray the Son of Man with a kiss?' And when those about him saw what would follow, they said, 'Lord, shall we strike with the sword?' And a certain one of them struck the servant of the high priest. But Jesus answered them and said, 'Suffer me thus far.' And touching the ear he healed it. And Jesus said to (those who had come against him, the chief priests and) the captains of the temple (and the elders), 'This is your hour and the power of darkness.'[1]

And arresting him, they brought him to the house of the high priest. [And the men who held him were mocking him. And they beat him and blindfolded him, and they kept asking him, saying, 'Play the prophet, who is he that struck you?' And they spoke many other things against him, railing at him.]

And when day came, the assembly of the elders of the people came together, the chief priests and the scribes, and they brought him to their Council, saying, 'If you are the Messiah, tell us.' And he said to them, 'If I tell you, you will not believe, and if I ask you, you will not answer. (But from now on the Son of Man will be seated at the right hand of the power of God.') And they all said, 'Are you then the Son of God?' And he said to them, 'You are saying that I am.' (And they said, 'What need have we

---

[1] See above, pp. 75f. [Ed.].

of further testimony? for we ourselves have heard from his mouth?')

And the whole company of them arose and brought him before Pilate. And they began to accuse him, saying, 'We found this man perverting our nation and forbidding to give tribute to Caesar and alleging himself to be Messiah, a king.' And Pilate said to the chief priests and the crowd, 'I find no case against this man.' But they were insistent, saying, 'He is stirring up the people, teaching throughout all Judaea, beginning from Galilee until this place.'

[Now when Pilate heard this, he asked if the man was a Galilean, and when he perceived that he belonged to Herod's jurisdiction, he sent him to Herod, for he was in Jerusalem in those days. Now when Herod saw Jesus he was very glad, since for a long time he had wanted to see him because he had heard about him and was hoping to see some sign done by him. And he questioned him at some length, but he answered him nothing. The chief priests and the scribes stood by accusing him vehemently. And Herod with his soldiers treated him with contempt and mocked him, arrayed him in a gorgeous robe, and sent him back to Pilate. And Herod and Pilate became friends with each other on that day, for before they had been at enmity with each other.

[Pilate then called together the chief priests and the rulers and the people and said to them, 'You brought this man to me as one who was perverting the people, and behold, after examining him in your presence I found in this man no crime among the things of which you accuse him; nor did Herod, for he has sent him back to me. In fact nothing deserving of death has been done by him. I therefore will scourge him and let him go.'] But they cried out in a body, saying, 'Away with this man, and release to us Barabbas', a man who for an insurrection in the city and for murder had been thrown into prison. Pilate therefore once more addressed them, desiring to release Jesus, but they shouted back, 'Crucify, crucify him.' And the third time he said to them, 'Why, what wrong has this man done? I have found in him no crime deserving of death. I will therefore scourge him and let him go.' But they were insistent with loud voices asking that he should be crucified. And their voices prevailed. And Pilate gave sentence that what they asked for should be done.

And there followed him a great crowd of the people and of women who bewailed and lamented him. And turning to them Jesus said to them, 'Daughters of Jerusalem, weep not for me, but weep for yourselves and your children, for behold days are coming in which men will say, "Blessed are the barren and the wombs that did not bear and the breasts which did not give suck." Then shall they begin to say to the mountains, "Fall upon us", and to the hills, "Cover us." For if they do these things when the wood is green, what will happen when it is dry?' And two others also, criminals, were led away to be put to death with him.

And when they came to the place called 'The Skull', there they crucified him and the criminals one on the right and the other on the left. And Jesus said, 'Father, forgive them; for they know not what they are doing.' And the people stood looking on. And the rulers mocked him saying, 'He saved others; let him save himself, if he is God's Anointed, his Chosen One.' The soldiers also mocked him, approaching him and offering him sour wine and saying, 'If you are the king of the Jews, save yourself.' And one of the criminals who hung with him railed at him, 'Are you not the Messiah? Save yourself and us.' But the other answered rebuking him, 'Do you not even fear God, seeing you are under the same condemnation? And we indeed justly, for we have received the due recompense for what we have done. But this man has done nothing wrong.' And he said, 'Jesus, remember me when you come into your kingdom.' And he said to him, 'Truly I say to you, today you will be with me in Paradise.'

And crying with a loud voice Jesus said, 'Father, into thy hands I commend my spirit.' And having said this he expired. And the centurion seeing what had happened glorified God saying, 'Certainly this man was innocent.' And all the crowds which had come together to see the sight, having beheld what had happened, beat their breasts and returned. [And the women who had come with him from Galilee followed and beheld the tomb and how his body was laid, and they returned and prepared spices and ointments.]

[And on the Sabbath they rested in accordance with the commandment. (But on the first day of the week, at early dawn, they came to the tomb bringing the spices which they had prepared. And they found the stone rolled away from the tomb, and entering in they found not the body.) And it came to pass that while they were perplexed about this, behold two men in dazzling apparel stood by them. And as they were affrighted and were bending their faces to the ground, they said to them, 'Why do you seek the living among the dead? Remember how he spoke to you while he was still in Galilee saying that the Son of Man must be delivered into the hands of sinful men and be crucified and rise on the third day.' And they remembered his words, and they returned and told all these things to the Eleven and to all the rest. And the rest of the women with them told these things to the apostles. And these words appeared to them to be idle talk, and they did not believe them.]

[And behold that very day two of them were journeying to a village called Emmaus about seven miles from Jerusalem. And they discussed one with the other all these things which had happened. And it came to pass that while they discussed and questioned together Jesus himself drew near and journeyed with them. And their eyes were held so that they did not recognise him. And he said to them, 'What are these words which you are exchanging with each other as you walk?' And they stood still with downcast faces. Then one of them, Cleopas by name, said to him, 'Are you the only person staying in Jerusalem who does not know what has happened there in these days?' And he said to them, 'What things?' And they said to him, 'The things concerning Jesus of Nazareth who was a prophet mighty in deed and word before God and all the people, how that our chief priests and rulers delivered him to the sentence of death, and crucified him. But we were hoping that it was he who should redeem Israel. Yes, and beside all these things, it is now the third day since these things happened. And some women of our company astonished us; they went early to the tomb, and not finding the body they came saying that they had seen a vision of angels, who said that he was alive. And some of those with us went away to the tomb and found it as the women had said, but him they saw not.' And he said to them, 'O foolish men and slow of heart to believe all that the prophets said! Was it not necessary that the Messiah should suffer these things and enter into his glory?' And beginning from Moses and all the prophets he interpreted to them in all the scriptures the things concerning himself.

[And they drew near to the village to which they were going, and he made as though he were going farther. And they constrained him, saying, 'Abide with us, for it is toward evening, and already the day is far spent.' And he entered in to abide with them. And it came to pass when he had reclined with them at table that, taking the bread, he gave thanks, and broke it, and distributed it to them. And their eyes were opened, and they recognised him; and he vanished out of their sight. And they said to each other, 'Was not our heart burning within us as he talked with us in the way, as he interpreted to us the scriptures?'

[And they arose that very hour and returned to Jerusalem and found the Eleven and those with them gathered together, who were saying, 'Of a truth the Lord is risen and has appeared to Simon.' And they recounted the things that had happened in the way, and how he was known to them in the breaking of the bread.]

[And as they were talking about these things he stood in the midst of them. And being terrified and full of fear they supposed that they were beholding a spirit. And he said to them, 'Why are you troubled and why do questionings arise in your heart? See my hands and my feet that it is I myself. Handle me and see, for a spirit has not flesh and bones as you see that I have.' And while they still disbelieved for joy, and wondered, he said to them, 'Have you anything here to eat?' And they gave him a piece of cooked fish, and receiving it he ate in their presence. Then he said to them, 'These are my words which I spoke to you while I was still with you, that it is necessary that all the things written about me in the law of Moses and the prophets and the psalms should be fulfilled.' Then he opened their mind to understand the scriptures. And he said to them, 'So it stands written that the Messiah should suffer and should rise from the dead on the third day, and that in his name repentance leading to the forgiveness of sins should be preached to all the nations – beginning from Jerusalem. And you are witnesses of these things. And behold I send forth unto you the promise of my Father. But stay in the city until you are clothed with power from on high.']

3. THE VALUE OF THE SPECIAL LUKAN
PASSION NARRATIVE:
HISTORICAL AND THEOLOGICAL

What is the value of the special Lukan Passion narrative? Is our investigation only an academic exercise or does it illuminate the historical and theological value of the narrative?

(a) Historical

(1) Light is undoubtedly thrown on the meaning of the Eucharist by the two narratives of Lk. xxii. 14–18 and Lk. xxii. 19–20. The former probably represents the form in which it was apprehended at Caesarea and the latter at Antioch. It is not surprising that the two are different in emphasis. It would be wrong, however, to set the one narrative against the other. Lk. xxii. 14–18 presents the eschatological aspect of the Last Supper and Lk. xxii. 19–20 reveals the saving activity of Jesus, but both are primitive. Caesarea did not necessarily dwell on the eschatological bearings of the Supper, and Antioch did not limit its interests to its soteriological significance. The basis of this claim is, on the one hand, the character of Lk. xxii. 14–18, and, if we accept the genuineness of Lk. xxii. 19*b*–20, the contents of Lk. xxii. 19–20, and, on the other hand, the words 'until he comes' in 1 Cor. xi. 26, for, although this phrase was added by St Paul, his reference to the Parousia in three Greek words suggests that the eschatological significance of the Eucharist was familiar to his readers. A belief that Jesus had spoken at the Supper of the Messianic Feast and of his blood poured out for many, available for the disciples here and now, lies behind both accounts.

The agreement of Luke's special source with John regarding the date of the Supper before the Passover is another point of historical importance. The testimony of the Fourth Gospel in xviii. 28 and xix. 14 is unambiguous and, as we have maintained,[1] in the words of Lk. xxii. 15, 'I have earnestly desired to eat this Passover meal before I suffer', Luke's source implied that the Supper preceded the Passover. If this interpretation is accepted, the agreement is a powerful argument in favour of the claim that the Supper was not the Passover.

---

[1] See above, p. 49.

(2) A second example of the superiority of the Lukan Passion narrative is its better account of the action of Judas. It supplies a more coherent account. Its representation might be explained as an attempt 'to spare the Twelve', especially as the source omits the prediction that Judas will betray Jesus and the account of Peter's denial, limiting itself to the declaration that Simon will fail to stand the test of Satan's sifting. Luke does not appear to know of the tradition of Judas's treacherous kiss[1] and avarice.[2] Judas leads the rabble and kisses Jesus, but his action is that of a confused disciple who apparently wishes to force the hand of Jesus. Luke contents himself with the explanation, as in John, that Satan entered into Judas, and the later traditions of deliberate treachery and greed are attempts to account for his deed. The Lukan Passion source stands nearer to the events as they happened.[3]

(3) The Passion source gives a better tradition in its account of the blow with the sword in the narrative of the arrest. In Mark the blow *follows* the arrest (xiv. 47) and is therefore naturally interpreted as an attempt to rescue the prisoner. In Lk. xxii. 50 and Jn. xviii. 10 it *precedes* the arrest and has the appearance of an attempt to resist it. This view is suggested by Rehkopf[4] who describes the blow as *ein Verteidigungsversuch* ('an attempt at defence'), and also by C. H. Dodd[5] who says that in Luke and John 'it...looks like an attempt to prevent it', whereas in Mark and Matt. it 'has the aspect of an attempted rescue'. Defence appears to be the more probable interpretation of the incident. The disciple is anxious to forestall arrest and so makes a wild move to prevent it. Jesus does not approve the act of his impetuous disciple. 'Suffer me thus far', he says, and heals the ear of the high priest's servant.[6] In John he commands Peter to put his sword into its sheath and says, 'Shall I not drink the cup which the Father has given me?'[7]

(4) Yet another example of the historical value of the Passion source is the account of the mocking. It is carried out by 'the

[1] Mk. xiv. 44f.   [2] Jn. xii. 6; Matt. xxvi. 15.
[3] See above, pp. 72–6.   [4] *LS*, pp. 65f.
[5] *HTFG*, p. 77.   [6] See above, pp. 74f.
[7] Jn. xviii. 11.

men who held him', in contrast with the Markan version which attributes it to members of the hierarchy – a most improbable suggestion. This claim is strongly supported if Streeter is right in contending on textual grounds that it is to Luke alone that we owe the references to blindfolding and to the question, 'Who is it that struck thee?'[1] The effect is to give distinctiveness to the account of the Lukan source in contrast with Mark, thus describing a coarse attempt to put the prophetic powers of Jesus to the test rather than, as in Mark, a challenge to play the prophet. Luke's account is much more vivid.

(5) A fifth example of the historical value of the Lukan Passion source is the reply of Jesus to the question, 'Are you the Messiah?' In Luke, Jesus parries the question and says, 'If I tell you, you will not believe, and if I ask you, you will not answer', and he declares that from now the Son of Man will be seated at the right hand of the power of God. When they all repeat the question, he replies, 'You say that I am', a reply which does not deny that he is the Messiah, but lays the onus of a reply upon his questioners. This agrees with Matt. xxvi. 64, where in answer to Caiaphas he says, 'Thou hast said so', and differs totally from the answer of Mk. xiv. 62, 'I am', unless perhaps we read σὺ εἶπας ὅτι ἐγώ εἰμι.[2] The Lukan reading stands much nearer to what Jesus actually said; it is not open to the charge of being a Christian formation. There is a parallel to the Lukan version in Jn. x. 24f., '"If you are the Messiah, tell us plainly." "I have told you", Jesus answered, "but you do not believe."' C. H. Dodd[3] is justified in claiming that John has used an independent form of tradition, although he connects it with the Feast of Tabernacles. In assigning the narrative of the examination before the priests to the following morning Luke is more likely to be correct than Mark who connects it with the night of the arrest.[4]

(6) The account of the examination before Pilate (Lk. xxiii. 1f., 4f.) is a further example of good historical tradition. It describes the political aspects of the accusation. The charge of perverting the nation, of forbidding to give tribute to Caesar, and of

---

[1] See above, p. 79.
[2] See V. Taylor, St Mark, p. 568.
[3] HTFG, pp. 91f.
[4] See above, pp. 81–4.

9-2

alleging himself to be Christos, a king, is more fully expressed
than in Mark, as well as the summary statement, 'they were
insistent, saying, "He is stirring up the people, teaching throughout all Judaea beginning from Galilee until this place."' The
account is highly condensed; Luke found it desirable to expand it
by the Markan insertion in xxiii. 3, in which Pilate asked Jesus,
'Are you the king of the Jews?' The Lukan account leaves the
impression of being based on sound historical tradition.

The historicity of the examination before Herod (xxiii. 6–16)
is more exposed to critical objection, since elsewhere we do not
learn of a quarrel between Pilate and Herod, but it is supported
by Luke's evident knowledge of the household of Herod (cf.
viii. 3), the early tradition implied in Acts iv. 25f. as a fulfilment
of Ps. ii. 2, and the statement 'he opened not his mouth' which is
in line with the Servant teaching of the same Acts passage.[1]
Streeter[2] has reason to suggest that strained relationships
between the two may have been due to the incident of Lk.
xiii. 1–5 which tells of Galileans (Herod's subjects) 'whose blood
Pilate had mingled with their sacrifices'.

The resumed examination before Pilate (xxiii. 18–25) is a
combination of historical fragments, including the Barabbas
story and the three attempts to release Jesus on the part of Pilate.
The attempts of Pilate may be motivated by the intention to
throw the responsibility for the condemnation of Jesus upon the
Jews, but it is confirmed by the independent testimony of John
and it agrees with the vacillation of the Roman governor. Pilate's
responsibility is pointedly affirmed by Luke himself when he says
that he released the man who for insurrection and murder had
been thrown into prison, whom they asked for, and gave up
Jesus to their will.

(7) The account of the crucifixion is artistic to a degree,
especially if we are right in recovering Luke's basic source, but he
has recognised its limitations by the additions drawn from Mark.
Its independence is shown by the form he has given to the
centurion's confession, 'Certainly this man was innocent', a form
which cannot be justly explained as a modification of Mark's
version, 'Truly this man was the Son of God.' Luke's account

[1] Cf. G. B. Caird, *St Luke*, p. 247.
[2] *Oxford Studies*, pp. 229–31.

reaches its climax in the centurion's confession and in the picture of the crowds beating their breasts when they saw what had happened. It is remarkable that when we set aside the passages which have considerable agreement with Mark, we are left with a continuous and well articulated account.

(8) The narratives of the resurrection raise the greatest historical problems. Whether Luke modified Mark's account of the visit of the women to the tomb is a point on which differences of opinion are inevitable. It is contrary to Luke's normal practice that he should amend the Markan narrative so drastically. I believe it is much more likely that he has followed and developed an independent source and has been to some extent influenced by a knowledge of Mark. The account of the journey to Emmaus follows a familiar plan visible in many of the resurrection narratives. Probably a simpler version of the story lies behind Luke's narrative, and many attempts have been made to recover it, but they remain very speculative and it is better to take the narrative as it stands. It contains many words characteristic of Luke's style. The narrative of the appearance to the Eleven stands nearer to the original source, but it is marked by theological and apologetic motives in the emphasis it lays on the bodily resurrection of Jesus.

(b) Theological

The theological character of the Passion source is in several respects distinctly primitive. This is true chiefly in two ways, the christological and the soteriological characteristics of the source. From the Third Gospel and Acts we can form a good impression of Luke's theology, and this differs from the theology implicit in his account of the Passion.

Christology

Luke's Christology is centred in his belief that Jesus is the Son of God.[1] Jesus is referred to as 'the Lord' in Luke fifteen times, all from sources, and frequently in Acts.[2] Elsewhere I have pointed

---

[1] 'Son of God', along with the allied names, 'the Son' and 'my Son', is found eleven times in Luke, but does not occur in passages belonging to the special source except in xxii. 70.

[2] See my Person of Christ in New Testament Teaching, p. 144. In Acts 'the

out that 'Lord' in its various combinations was by preference the habitual usage of primitive Christianity.[1] It is especially characteristic of the post-resurrection period. The vocabulary of Sonship, with its correlative 'Father', and the use of the Servant conception, were adopted by Jesus and are characteristic of Luke, but influenced by his sources and current usage he used the name 'Lord' freely in Acts. His earlier preference was for the concept of Sonship, and stands in contrast to the usage of his special source in the Third Gospel. Distinctiveness belongs to this source in its use of 'Lord'.[2] A. R. C. Leaney has observed that Luke's theme is the reign of Christ.[3] But βασιλεύς used of Jesus is found only five times in the Gospel and once in Acts (xvii. 7). It is significant that all the Lukan examples in the Gospel, except xix. 38, are in the Passion narrative,[4] so that, as far as it goes, this usage is characteristic of his sources rather than of Luke himself.

More important is the use of the name 'Son of Man'. Rehkopf[5] shows on linguistic grounds that the title is characteristic of the Lukan sources, and not of Luke himself.[6] Apart from passages taken from Mark, Q, and L, he never speaks of Jesus as 'the Son of Man'. The Passion narrative depicts Jesus as the Servant of the Lord without using the name, as in iii. 22 and xxii. 37, but Luke refers to him as παῖς in Acts iii. 13, 26; iv. 27, 30, and in the story of the Ethiopian eunuch (Acts viii. 27–39).

Luke's Christology is a Son–Servant Christology, but he does not impose this usage on his special source, which reflects a more primitive point of view. The evangelist left his sources as he found them, not modifying them by his distinctive teaching.

Lord', along with 'the Lord Jesus', 'the Lord Jesus Christ', and 'our Lord Jesus Christ', occurs forty-two times, but 'the Son of God' and 'my Son' once each.

[1] *Op. cit.* p. 148.
[2] Cf. Streeter, *FG*, pp. 212–14.
[3] *St Luke*, pp. 34–7.
[4] Lk. xxiii. 2, 3, 37, 38 (vv. 2 and 37 belong to the special source, vv. 3 and 38 to Mark; see above, p. 119).
[5] *LS*, p. 97.
[6] As we have seen (p. 25), Rehkopf claims that out of twenty-five or twenty-six examples seven are taken over from Mark and all the rest (eighteen or nineteen) from Q and L, while Acts has a single example (vii. 56).

Soteriology

Here again we can trace a difference between Luke and his sources. He describes the work of Christ as pre-eminently an act of obedience to the Father's will. But he does not depict the work of Christ in terms of sacrifice or emphasise his atoning ministry. These ideas appear in his sources, especially the Passion narrative.[1] Here, if we accept Lk. xxii. 19*b*–20 as a genuine element in Luke, he describes Christ's Body as 'given for you' and his Blood as 'poured out for you', and speaks of the Eucharistic Cup as 'the new covenant made by blood'. It is significant that Luke omits the Markan saying, 'The Son of Man came not to be served, but to serve, and to give his life a ransom for many' (Mk. x. 45). His parallel to this saying is the simpler declaration, 'I am in the midst of you as he who serves' (Lk. xxii. 27). He also omits the cry of dereliction (Mk. xv. 34) and portrays Jesus as commending his spirit to the Father (Lk. xxiii. 46).

It is not necessary to regard the two representations of the work of Christ as mutually exclusive. Luke has taken over the theology of his sources and makes it his own. This fact is manifest in Acts. Here Jesus is described as 'a man approved of God' (ii. 22), who 'went about doing good' (x. 38), and men are exhorted to repent and turn to God, that their sins may be blotted out, so that 'a time of recovery' may be granted to them by the Lord (iii. 19). Jesus 'must be received into heaven until the time of universal restoration, of which God spoke by his holy prophets' (iii. 21). Jesus is 'the saviour' (xiii. 23), and 'there is no other name under heaven granted to men, by which we must be saved' (iv. 12). Through him every one who has faith is acquitted of everything for which there was no acquittal under the law of Moses (xiii. 39). Christians belong to the Church of God which he won for himself by 'the blood of his own' (xx. 28). In the light of his Gospel and Acts we can see Luke's soteriology expanding and coming to greater maturity.

If we consider together the historical and the theological characteristics of the special Lukan Passion source, we find that it throws a welcome light upon the course of early Christian

---

[1] It should be pointed out that the ideas in question belong to the 'pre-Lukan liturgical source' rather than to the special Passion source. See above, p. 126 n. 2 [Ed.].

history and development; we enter the 'tunnel period' and see something of primitive Christianity as far back as the forties. Doubtless Luke has modified his sources, but to a large extent we can distinguish between what he has received and what he has added or modified. Our knowledge of Christianity ten years or so after the time of Christ is increased and deepened. These are not small gains, and we owe them in large measure to Luke's Passion source.

BIBLIOGRAPHY

Bacon, B. W. *Studies in Matthew* (New York and London, 1930).

Balmforth, H. *The Gospel According to St Luke* (Oxford, 1930).

Bammel, E., ed. *The Trial of Jesus: Cambridge Studies in honour of C. F. D. Moule* (London, 1970).

Barbour, R. S. 'Gethsemane in the Tradition of the Passion', *NTS*, xvi (1970), 231ff.

Bartlet, J. V. 'The Sources of St Luke's Gospel', in *Oxford Studies in the Synoptic Problem*, ed. W. Sanday (Oxford, 1911), pp. 315–62.

Billerbeck, P. *See* Strack, H. L.

Black, M. *An Aramaic Approach to the Gospels and Acts*, 3rd edn (Oxford, 1967).

Borgen, P. 'John and the Synoptics in the Passion Narrative', *NTS*, v (1959), 246ff.

Bultmann, R. *The History of the Synoptic Tradition*, Eng. trans. J. Marsh (Oxford, 1963).

Burkitt, F. C. *The Gospel History and its Transmission* (Edinburgh, 1906).

'The Use of Mark in the Gospel according to Luke', in *The Beginnings of Christianity*, ed. K. Lake and F. J. Foakes Jackson (London, 1920–33), II, 106–20.

Buse, S. I. 'St John and the Marcan Passion Narrative', *NTS*, IV (1958), 215ff.

'St John and the Passion Narratives of St Matthew and St Luke', *NTS*, VII (1960), 65ff.

Bussmann, W. *Synoptische Studien*, I–III (Halle, 1925–31).

Cadbury, H. J. *The Style and Literary Method of Luke* (Cambridge, Mass., 1919–20).

Caird, G. B. *The Gospel of St Luke*, The Pelican Gospel Commentaries (London, 1963).

Clarke, W. K. L. 'The Use of the Septuagint in Acts', in *The Beginnings of Christianity*, ed. K. Lake and F. J. Foakes Jackson (London, 1920–33), II, 66–105.

Creed, J. M. *The Gospel According to St Luke* (London, 1930).

'"L" and the Structure of the Lucan Gospel', *ET*, xlvi, 101–7.

'The Supposed "Proto-Lucan" Narrative of the Trial before Pilate: A Rejoinder', *ET*, xlvi, 378f.

Dalman, G. *The Words of Jesus*, Eng. trans. D. M. Kay (Edinburgh, 1902).

Jesus–Jeshua, Eng. trans. P. P. Levertoff (London, 1929).

Davey, F. N. *See* Hoskyns, E. C.

Dibelius, M. *From Tradition to Gospel*, Eng. trans. B. L. Woolf (London, 1934).

Dodd, C. H. *The Parables of the Kingdom* (London, 1935).

Historical Tradition in the Fourth Gospel (Cambridge, 1963).

Dodd, C. H. (*cont.*)
'The Appearances of the Risen Christ: An Essay in Form-Criticism of the Gospels', in *Studies in the Gospels*, ed. D. E. Nineham (Oxford, 1955).
Easton, B. S. *The Gospel According to St Luke* (Edinburgh, 1926).
Ellis, E. E. *The Gospel of Luke* (London, 1966).
Farrer, A. *A Study in Mark* (Westminster, 1951).
Feine, P. *Eine vorkanonische Überlieferung des Lukas* (Gotha, 1891).
Fiebig, P. *Der Erzählungsstil der Evangelien* (Leipzig, 1925).
Geden, A. S. *See* Moulton, W. F.
Gilmour, S. McL. 'A Critical Re-examination of Proto-Luke', *JBL*, LXVII (1948), 143–52.
'The Gospel According to St Luke' (*Interpreters' Bible*, VIII; New York and Nashville, 1951).
Grant, F. C. *The Growth of the Gospels* (New York, 1933).
The Gospels: Their Origin and Their Growth (London, 1957).
Hahn, F. *Christologische Hoheitstitel* (Göttingen, 1963).
Harnack, A. *Luke the Physician* (London, 1907).
The Sayings of Jesus (London, 1908).
The Acts of the Apostles (London, 1909).
The Date of the Acts and of the Synoptic Gospels (London, 1911).
Hawkins, J. C. *Horae Synopticae*, 2nd edn (Oxford, 1909).
'Three Limitations to St Luke's Use of St Mark's Gospel', in *Oxford Studies in the Synoptic Problem*, ed. W. Sanday (Oxford, 1911), pp. 29–94.
Holtzmann, H. J. *Die Synoptiker* (Tübingen, 1901).
Hort, F. J. A. *See* Westcott, B. F.
Hoskyns, E. C. and Davey, F. N. *The Riddle of the New Testament* (London, 1931).
Howard, W. F. *See* Moulton, J. H.
Huck, A. *A Synopsis of the First Three Gospels*, 9th edn, Eng. trans. F. L. Cross (Oxford, 1936).
Hunkin, J. W. 'The Composition of the Third Gospel, with Special Reference to Canon Streeter's Theory of Proto-Luke', *JTS*, XXVIII (1927), 250–62.
The New Testament: A Conspectus (London, 1950).
Hunter, A. M. *Interpreting the New Testament 1900–1950* (London, 1951).
Jackson, F. J. Foakes. *See* Lake, K.
Jeremias, J. *The Parables of Jesus*, 6th edn, Eng. trans. S. H. Hooke (London, 1963).
The Eucharistic Words of Jesus, 3rd edn, Eng. trans. N. Perrin (London, 1966).
'Perikopen-Umstellungen bei Lukas', *NTS*, IV (1958), 115ff.
Jülicher, A. *Die Gleichnisreden Jesu*, I–II, 2nd edn (Tübingen, 1910).
Kenyon, F. G. *Recent Developments in the Textual Criticism of the Greek Bible* (London, 1933).
The Text of the Greek Bible (London, 1937).
Kilpatrick, G. D. 'Luke xxii. 19b–20', *JTS*, XLVII (1946), 49–56.
'Scribes, Lawyers and Lucan Origins', *JTS*, NS, I (1950), 56–60.
Klostermann, E. *Das Lukasevangelium*, 2nd edn (Tübingen, 1929).

Knox, W. L. *The Sources of the Synoptic Gospels*, I–II (Cambridge, 1953–7).

Kümmel, W. G. *Introduction to the New Testament*, Eng. trans. A. J. Mattill, Jr. (London, 1966).

Lake, K. *The Historical Evidence for the Resurrection of Jesus Christ* (London, 1907).

and Jackson, F. J. Foakes, ed., *The Beginnings of Christianity*, I–V (London, 1920–33).

Leaney, A. R. C. *The Gospel According to St Luke* (London, 1958).

Review of *Die lukanische Sonderquelle*, by F. Rehkopf, *JTS*, NS, XII (1961), 74ff.

Legg, S. C. E. *Nouum Testamentum Graece: Euangelium secundum Marcum* (Oxford, 1935).

Lightfoot, R. H. *History and Interpretation in the Gospels* (London, 1935).

The Gospel Message of St Mark (Oxford, 1950).

Luce, H. K. *The Gospel According to S. Luke* (Cambridge, 1933).

Manson, T. W. *A Companion to the Bible* (Edinburgh, 1939).

The Sayings of Jesus (London, 1949).

Manson, W. *The Gospel of Luke* (London, 1930).

Meyer, E. *Ursprung und Anfänge des Christentums*, I–III (Berlin, 1921–3).

Micklem, E. R. *Miracles and the New Psychology* (Oxford, 1922).

Milligan, G. *See* Moulton, J. H.

Moffatt, J. *Introduction to the Literature of the New Testament*, 3rd edn (Edinburgh, 1918).

Moulton, J. H. *The Christian Religion in the Study and the Street* (London, 1919).

and Howard, W. F. *A Grammar of New Testament Greek*, I–II (Edinburgh, 1906–29).

and Milligan, G. *The Vocabulary of the Greek Testament* (London, 1914–29).

Moulton, W. F. and Geden, A. S. *A Concordance to the Greek Testament*, 3rd edn (Edinburgh, 1926).

Nineham, D. E. *The Gospel of St Mark*, The Pelican Gospel Commentaries (London, 1963).

ed. *Studies in the Gospels: Essays in Memory of R. H. Lightfoot* (Oxford, 1955).

Otto, R. *The Kingdom of God and the Son of Man*, 2nd edn, Eng. trans. F. V. Filson and B. L. Woolf (London, 1943).

Parker, P. *The Gospel Before Mark* (Chicago, 1953).

Perry, A. M. *Sources of Luke's Passion Narrative* (Chicago, 1920).

'Luke's Disputed Passion-Source', *ET*, XLVI, 256–60.

Plummer, A. *The Gospel According to S. Luke*, 4th edn (Edinburgh, 1901).

Rehkopf, F. *Die lukanische Sonderquelle, Ihr Umfang und Sprachgebrauch* (Tübingen, 1959).

Sanday, W., ed. *Oxford Studies in the Synoptic Problem* (Oxford, 1911).

Schneider, G. *Verleugnung, Verspottung, und Verhör Jesu nach Lukas 22. 54–71* (München, 1969).

Schramm, T. *Der Markus-Stoff bei Lukas* (Cambridge, 1971).

Schürmann, H. *Quellenkritische Untersuchung des lukanischen Abendmahlsberichtes Lk. xxii. 7–38:* I *Der Paschamahlbericht Lk. xxii.* (7–14), 15–18; II *Der Einsetzungsbericht Lk. xxii. 19–20;* III *Jesu Abschiedsrede Lk. xxii. 21–38* (Münster, 1953–7).

Schürmann, H. (*cont.*)

Traditionsgeschichtliche Untersuchungen zu den synoptischen Evangelien (Düsseldorf, 1968).

Sparks, H. F. D. 'St Luke's Transpositions', *NTS*, III (1957), 219–23.

'The Semitisms of St Luke's Gospel', *JTS*, XLIV (1943), 129–38.

Stanton, V. H. *The Gospels as Historical Documents*, I–III (Cambridge, 1903–20).

Strack, H. L. and Billerbeck, P. *Kommentar zum Neuen Testament aus Talmud und Midrasch*, I–IV (München, 1922–8).

Streeter, B. H. Essays in *Oxford Studies in the Synoptic Problem*, ed. W. Sanday (Oxford, 1911), pp. 139–231, 423–36.

The Four Gospels: A Study of Origins (London, 1924).

Taylor, V. 'Proto-Luke', *ET*, XXXIII, 250–2.

'The Value of the Proto-Luke Hypothesis', *ET*, XXXVI, 476f.

Behind the Third Gospel: A Study of the Proto-Luke Hypothesis (Oxford, 1926).

The First Draft of St Luke's Gospel (London, 1927).

'Is the Proto-Luke Hypothesis Sound?', *JTS*, XXIX (1928), 147–55.

'Professor J. M. Creed and the Proto-Luke Hypothesis', *ET*, XLVI, 236–8.

'Professor Creed's Rejoinder', *ET*, XLVI, 379.

The Gospels: A Short Introduction, 9th edn (London, 1960).

The Formation of the Gospel Tradition, 2nd edn (London, 1935).

Jesus and His Sacrifice (London, 1937).

The Atonement in New Testament Teaching (London, 1940).

Forgiveness and Reconciliation (London, 1941).

'The Proto-Luke Hypothesis: A Rejoinder', *ET*, LIV, 219–22.

The Gospel According to St Mark, 2nd edn (London, 1966).

The Names of Jesus (London, 1953).

The Life and Ministry of Jesus (London, 1954).

The Person of Christ in New Testament Teaching (London, 1958).

'Important Hypotheses Reconsidered: The Proto-Luke Hypothesis', *ET*, LXVII, 12–16.

'Sources of the Lukan Passion Narrative', *ET*, LXVIII, 95.

'Modern Issues in Biblical Studies: Methods of Gospel Criticism', *ET*, LXXI, 68–72.

The Text of the New Testament: A Short Introduction (London, 1961).

'Theologians of our Time: Heinz Schürmann', *ET*, LXXIV, 77–81.

'Theologians of our Time: Friedrich Rehkopf', *ET*, LXXIV, 262–6.

'The Narrative of the Crucifixion', *NTS*, VIII (1962), 333f.

'Rehkopf's List of Words and Phrases Illustrative of Pre-Lukan Speech Usage', *JTS*, NS XV (1964), 59–62.

New Testament Essays (London, 1970).

Vööbus, A. 'A New Approach to the Problem of the Shorter and Longer Text in Luke', *NTS*, XV (1969), 457ff.

Weiss, B. *The Life of Jesus*, I–III, Eng. trans. J. W. Hope (Edinburgh, 1883).

Die Evangelien des Markus und Lukas (Göttingen, 1901).

Die Quellen der synoptischen Überlieferung (Leipzig, 1908).

Weiss, J. *Die Schriften des Neuen Testaments*, 3rd edn (Göttingen, 1917).

BIBLIOGRAPHY

Wellhausen, J. *Das Evangelium Lucae* (Berlin, 1904).

Einleitung in die drei ersten Evangelien, 2nd edn (Berlin, 1911).

Westcott, B. F. and Hort, F. J. A. *The New Testament in the Original Greek, Introduction and Appendix* (Cambridge and London, 1882).

Williams, C. S. C. *Alterations to the Text of the Synoptic Gospels and Acts* (Oxford, 1951).

'The Synoptic Problem', in *Peake's Commentary on the Bible,* revised edn (London, 1962), pp. 748–55.

Winter, P. *On the Trial of Jesus* (Berlin, 1961).

'The Treatment of his Sources by the Third Evangelist', *Studia Theologica,* VIII, ii (1954), 138–72.

Review of *Der Paschamahlbericht,* by H. Schürmann, *NTS,* II (1956), 207ff.

Review of *Der Einsetzungsbericht* and *Jesu Abschiedsrede,* by H. Schürmann, *NTS,* IV (1958), 223ff.

INDEX

INDEX